My Story

A Memoir

Don Nordine

InspiringVoices®

I want to give thanks to Larry and Carol Schatz, lifetime missionaries with Wycliffe Bible Translators, who helped edit and fit this book together.

My Story

Copyright © 2014 Don Nordine.

Inspiring Voices books may be ordered through booksellers or by contacting:

Inspiring Voices
1663 Liberty Drive
Bloomington, IN 47403
www.inspiringvoices.com
1 (866) 697-5313

Because of the dynamic nature of the Internet, any web addresses or links contained in this book may have changed since publication and may no longer be valid. The views expressed in this work are solely those of the author and do not necessarily reflect the views of the publisher, and the publisher hereby disclaims any responsibility for them.

ISBN: 978-1-4624-0970-9 (sc)
ISBN: 978-1-4624-0971-6 (e)

Library of Congress Control Number: 2014909235

Printed in the United States of America.

Inspiring Voices rev. date: 06/30/2014

This book is dedicated to all the people who came from Oklahoma and back east to California to find work and a better life. My hope is that it will give them some tools to achieve that better life financially and spiritually.

Table of Contents

Foreword

*"Trust in the Lord with all your heart, and do
not lean on your own understanding.
In all your ways acknowledge Him and He
will direct your paths."* Proverbs 3:5-6

"The work of a man's hand comes back to him" Proverbs 12:14

Two words describe Don Nordine, those two words are "directed" and "worker". He is a living illustration of what King Solomon wrote about three thousand years ago.

In this book, Don's story, you will read of a life that was truly directed by God. Time after time you will read of people and opportunities that God brought into Don's life as He built this man into the person he was created to be.

Buildings were made available for them to live in. Jobs were there, even at low pay, to help them get through. People helped him right when he needed them most. He was taught what he needed to know. Reading this story is like watching a puzzle being put together. It is a story of a life directed by God, and the final picture, when all the pieces have been identified and put in place, is a picture of a beautiful life blessed by God.

And, what was Don's response all along the way?

(1) He worked hard at everything he did so he could provide for his family and take advantage of those opportunities that God gave to him.
(2) He trusted God even in the most difficult times, never quitting, but always moving ahead in faith
(3) He acknowledged God with his life and efforts and became involved in the church and sharing what he had learned with others.

This book has three stories: the first is of a family, a large family and their journey. It's a story that modern day families will marvel at. It's about lots of kids, no money, living wherever they can… making it.

The second story is Don's faith journey and how God used and blessed him. It is a strong testimony of God's direction and faithfulness.

The third story is a fun walk through years of public signs that share truths about God and His relationship with man. Those signs that Don put up have some powerful reminders and every one of them is worth thinking about.

I have known Don for over 40 years and am happy to share this book, his secret for success. His secret is wrapped up in those two words… he's a worker who is directed by God!

Dr. Ron Cline
Reach Beyond Global Ambassador

Chapter 1

The Years of My Childhood

MY EARLY YEARS

I was born in the charity ward of the University Hospital in Oklahoma City, Oklahoma, on March 15, 1937.

My family had fallen on hard times. I was the last of nine children. The family lived in the back of a store building that had been the dry goods store that my mother, Pearl Sussie Brown Nordine, and father, Jeff Ollie Nordine, had run for years.

Sometime when I was a year or so old, my dad was taken to the hospital with an illness and never returned home. I recall a kind older man called Uncle Mike Moses staying at our place. I remember sitting on his lap, drinking coffee with him. As I recall, Uncle Mike passed away while we lived at 501 North Eastern Avenue. While living on Eastern, I had a doll. I know boys are not supposed to have dolls, but someone gave me this doll, Patsy. I don't recall her after we moved to our next home on a ten-acre farm. I tried to get my granddaughters to name their dolls Patsy, but they never did.

My mother worked for the Bushey family, who operated a chicken house on our street. They lived around the corner and

Mrs. Tennison, who was Mrs. Bushey's mother, took a liking to me and taught me to write my name and do some simple reading. I believe they were Catholic because when my older brother, Elbert, was very sick, Mrs. Bushey had their priest come and pray for him. As the story goes, when the baby woke up he was saying, "Jesus." This is a hand-me-down story, as it was before my time.

World War II was going on and things were rationed. We saved the vegetable cans and they were picked up for the war effort. Those early days of salvaging cans and other things from the trash made an impression on me, as I still salvage a good deal. During that time, I also remember getting the measles. I was very sick and when I got up, my legs seemed to be so weak I could barely walk.

There was a fairground down the street, and we kids would watch the fair come in and unload. One of my older brothers, Burl, joined up with them at age 14 and never came back home for long after that. He was a concessionaire all his life except for a short time when he was a jockey. Many years later my sister Harmeda and her husband, Fred, joined my wife and me to go see Burl before he died. He was in the veterans' hospital in Tampa, Florida. I asked a couple men I knew from my prayer group to pray for me before I left for the trip. God prepared the way. Nancy's aunt and uncle lived in Tampa, and we told them about Burl and they went to see him before we got there. They were Christian folks and visited with him. As I recall, on our second visit, I asked Burl if he would like to pray to receive Christ Jesus as his Savior. He said yes, and I went through the plan and prayer with him. Three days later he died. I spoke at his funeral, and the pastor from Nancy's aunt's church also spoke.

My first recollection of school was going to kindergarten at Bath school. Miss Lisa was my teacher. We had little rugs and took naps each day. One day I was running in the room and fell and got a cut above my left eye. I seem to have always been running, but one time I really stopped. It was a cold winter day, ice everywhere. I am not sure what prompted me, but as I was going into the school, which had pipe rails on the steps, I stuck my tongue out and it stuck to the rail. Well, it was only for a few seconds, but the memory stuck with me. I should have learned then to not let your tongue get you into trouble.

When I was about six years old, my mother married a man named Ralph Downey, who had six or seven children, four still at home. Their mother had died in childbirth. My mother and stepfather sold our old store building and purchased ten acres about twenty-five miles out from the city. Ralph Downey was a rough horseman who graded yard, etc.

When I was in first grade, we had to walk about half a mile to the bus stop for school, forging a small creek on the way. The school was called Bridge Creek, and it had outside plumbing. The drinking fountains were pipes with holes drilled in them, and the older kids would hand pump the water. When the pipe was full, water squirted out the holes and made a fountain.

The bus was very old and we city kids never liked the country school. I was the youngest, and we often went as far as the creek and turned around and went back home and played. Mom and our stepfather were not home during the day as they went to Oklahoma City to work. We finally just all quit going to school that year, so I quit school in the first grade!

Well, if you are going to choose a stepdad, don't pick a mule skinner. That's what they call someone who drives mules. The next year we tried the same trick. The creek was up one day, and we turned around and went back home. But this time our mule skinner stepfather came out to meet us with his horsewhip. That was the end of our hooky days. That creek was no longer a problem!

On one of those hooky days, though, my brother Carl,

stepsister Irene, and stepbrother Jim went across the field and smoked hay straws, and the haystack went up in flames. The haystack burned to the ground, and our neighbor was waiting for our stepdad as he came by on his way home. We had cleaned the place and gone to bed early. It seems he knew the guilty ones and pulled them out of bed and horsewhipped them good. Smoking was not on my agenda after that. I never got the whipping, but I got the message.

We were very poor and often ate cold gravy sandwiches with a slice of onion and lots of beans and potatoes. The neighbor who lost his haystack also lost a rooster, and I think my mom had something to do with that. All I remember is eating roast rooster and not seeing that rooster along our fence anymore.

My sister Fredia had married Edwin Weaver, an army buddy of my brother Ollie, and when the war was over, they came and lived on the ten acres with us. We made the garage into their living quarters.

The place behind our property had an apricot tree and I loved apricots. We kids would crawl over the fence and help ourselves to apricots. On one occasion, I climbed over the fence and up into the apricot tree. I ate apricots and more apricots; they were just about the sweetest fruit I had ever eaten. After filling my stomach with apricots and maybe a few worms, I went home. I was soon so sick that I could see apricots with my eyes closed. Mom and Downey, my stepdad, came home and they laid me on their bed. I soon was out. I still love apricots.

My sister's husband, Edwin, hired me to bring in wood at one cent a load and I soon had two dollars—enough to buy a pair of leather gloves. Edwin and I would go squirrel hunting. I would climb the tree and flush them out and Edwin would catch them. We built a cage for them. Squirrel meat was good food in those days. We were cotton pullers and, as I recall, I wasn't given my regular cotton gloves, but had to wear my new leather gloves, and they were soon worn out. That was a bad investment.

I got along okay with all my family and my mom and stepdad. I was (and still am) gifted in fixing things and the kids sometime called me Mastermind, because I could fix things and I often gave advice to others, sometimes unwanted. Even though there were six of us kids at home, I was somewhat of a loner.

During the war, my brother Ollie wrote me letters, which were censored. Somehow he thought I was special and wanted me to be called Joe, so Joe became my nickname. When I graduated from high school, the principal had me down as Joe Donald. I went to him and explained that Joe was just a nickname.

My mother often prayed with us at bedtime, saying the Lord's Prayer and the Twenty-third Psalm, so prayer became a part of my life at an early age. I recall that when World War II ended, I went out and knelt down by a little stone bridge in our yard and thanked the Lord that Ollie, who was injured in the war, and Edwin were coming home. Once when stepbrother Ralph was bitten by a black widow and hospitalized, we all gathered and prayed for him. A few days later he was okay. Then I lost my pocketknife, maybe at age eight, and I prayed, and it was in my pocket the next morning! In that case I am not sure it was a blessing, as I carried that knife partly as a weapon.

Our stepfather told us boys not to let anyone push us around and if we got beaten up at school, to just get some leverage, like a stick, knife, or bat, and even the score. Once a bigger boy called me some names, and I took after him with a broken bat. The teacher, Mr. Leathers, came out and broke the paddle over my butt, so I sort of started to get the message.

Having bigger brothers had its advantages. Once when we were watching a ballgame, I got into a fight with a bigger lad, and he hit me so hard I saw sparks. Well, big brother Carl cleaned his plow, as we farmers would say.

We lived on the ten acres for a few years and then moved to a larger farm where we were sharecroppers. From there we moved to a two-room shack, and from there to a 16' x 16' army tent on the road, pulling cotton from Western Oklahoma to New Mexico. In New Mexico, we picked cotton rather than pulling it. In other words, we picked the cotton out of the burr, rather than pulling off the whole burr with the cotton in it. It takes a lot more cotton without the burr to get the same weight. Our winter in New Mexico we boys slept in a boxcar for a while. Then my stepfather got a job where we were given a two-room house.

I have some great memories of our time near Hagerman. The fields were irrigated, and the reservoirs had warm artesian water flowing in them in the cold winter. With the rising steam and the wild geese and ducks and farm geese, it was a nature picture I still remember. When the geese hatched their eggs and those little goslings followed them around the ponds, it was a beautiful sight. The year we were in New Mexico we went to the Carlsbad Caverns, and that was the most magnificent sight I had ever seen.

I was in the fourth grade and our teacher read out of the Bible to us each day. At that time I was still an unsaved lad who thought he was a bit tough. I got in a fight with a local boy in my grade and won. Well, a few days later Carl, stepbrother Jim, and I were riding our bikes to town. Carl had his own bike, while Jim and I shared a bike. One of our bikes had a flat and we stopped and asked some people for help. Well, they turned out to be the family of the boy I had beaten up at school. They not only would not help, but they pulled out a knife and came after us. We left in a hurry, flat tire and all. We knew we were outnumbered.

We worked as farm laborers for forty cents an hour. On one farm, they had a lead man and we were expected to keep up with him. My stepfather came up to me and said, "Burn him up, Joe." I would hoe up behind him and call out, "Move over, Big'un."

Then he would come up behind me and call out, "Move over, Little'un." At the break, he asked my stepfather, "What do you feed these kids?" His reply was, "Blackjack brush."

One of my most embarrassing moments was when we were playing cops and robbers with the neighbors' kids and they tied me up to a truck bumper. That was okay till I had to potty. I managed to get my pants down and pottied, still tied up to the bumper. Well, it so happened that the neighbor lady came out and saw me. She was kind and understanding, but I was terribly embarrassed.

As the summer ended we loaded our stuff in a trailer and headed back to Oklahoma. We pulled cotton in Vinson and Reed. A farmer liked our work, and our stepfather made a deal to sharecrop for him on the halves. "On the halves" means that the owner furnishes the land, tractor, and other tools, the sharecropper supplies all the labor, and the profits are split. That winter we lived in Alex Thomson's house and sharecropped. Alex bought a new Ford pickup and I recall he said it cost a thousand dollars.

We had a red bulldog named Queen that would kill chickens. I recall Mom taking a stick to her. The dog gave up killing chickens and became Mom's dog. We had a small, screw-tail bulldog, Tippy. When the big red came in heat, our landlord's big collie came visiting. Well, that didn't set well with little Tippy. Tippy attacked the big collie, and the collie chewed him up pretty bad. Tippy lay around half dead. Then the big collie came back to pay Queen another visit. To make a long story short, Tippy died trying to defend his lady. Little Tippy didn't have a big brother to defend him like I did. I should have learned a lesson—size up the task before you make your move.

That was the year I purchased a horse for ten dollars, but my stepfather said I had to buy the feed—which he owned. My brother Carl used his ten dollars to purchase a nice bike.

Feed for my horse was ten cents a bundle. Well, it wasn't long till my feed bill was ten dollars, and my stepfather repossessed my horse and sold it. My brother's bike was still nice. He rode it and I walked.

On that farm Mom got a big black pot and made soap, using lye and fats as I recall. We got our water from a well with a rope and bucket.

**This is me when I was about eleven years old.
I was called Joe in those days.**

After that we purchased a farm a few miles away from our landlord. At our new farm we had 160 acres, a barn, a four-room house, a dugout cellar, and a well. The well soon went dry and we drilled another one. We raised corn, cantaloupes, peas, watermelons, cotton, cucumbers, peanuts, and forty acres of pasture for the cows. My stepbrother Jim and I were expected to feed the hogs and bring in the cows for milking. I recall that once Jim and I were going for the cows. Jim was up ahead a good ways when I stumbled on something. I looked down and saw the biggest, longest rattlesnake I ever saw in the wild. I was lucky. I jumped and called to Jim. He came back and we stoned the snake; one of us would watch it while the other one went for more stones. We took it to the house and showed the family.

One year our stepdad gave Jim and me a small plot of land to raise peanuts. As soon as they were planted and started to come up, in came a storm and washed out our crop. Oklahoma is noted for tornados; the Bridge Creek, Newcastle, and Centralvue schools have all blown away. My stepfather made us go to the dugout cellar when it looked like a storm. I hated those dugouts. The lantern smoke would kill more people than the storms. On my junior high graduation day, a storm came up and we all went to the dugout.

Our house on Ladessa Road

Once, when we did not go to the dugout, we did get such a bad storm that it blew our neighbors' house away. I recall sitting on a bench against the wall of our house. The wall was moving,

9

but somehow the house never went. I believe we were the last people to live in that old house, which was still there when I visited thirty years later.

After we had been on our farm a few years, a storm came and wiped out the crops. We stayed there another year or so, and then since we couldn't pay for it, the nice old landlord asked us to leave. On this farm we mostly worked out as farm laborers for others.

The six kids: (L to R top) Irene Downey, Jim Downey Harmeda Nordine, Carl Nordine, (bottom) Joe Donald Nordine, Margaret Downey, our dog Queen

We were the best cotton pullers around. One year we worked with a middle-aged man named Tiny who put us to shame, and we soon learned to be even better cotton pullers. I watched the pro and copied his style. I finally got up to 1,051 pounds for my high day of pulling cotton. That is about three times what an average man pulls. We were paid two cents a pound. Once you have pulled cotton for a living, most other jobs seem like a piece of cake.

I attended Centralvue School and was active in 4-H Club, becoming president and raising chickens and pigs. When I was sixteen, I got my driver's license and often drove the school bus for day games. At our school a bus-driving job paid forty dollars a month, but in my junior year I drove just to get out of class.

While we were living on the farm on Ladessa Road, one of our big sows had a large litter of pigs. One was a runt, so we took him out of the pen and bottle-fed him. We called him Billy. We didn't have running water in the house there, or hot and cold water. We had a long galvanized tub that we took baths in on Saturday evening, before going to town to a movie. We often set our galvanized tub out in the sun to warm the water. Once when we came back, our little pet pig, Billy, was in the tub enjoying a bath. I cannot recall whether or not we changed the water. Being the second from the bottom of the roster, I generally had to use secondhand water anyway. We finally sold Billy; we didn't have the heart to kill and eat him.

We did kill hogs and chickens on the farm and eat them. One year the 4-H Club had a chicken program where a merchant in town would buy fifty chicks and give them to a 4-H member. When they were grown, the clubber would give three chickens to the merchant who had purchased the chicks and keep the rest. I got fifty and Carl got fifty. We didn't have a house for the chickens, so I saw an old flatbed truck body out in the yard and, with some scrap tin and wood, I made a chicken house. I wired it from the smokehouse and made a brooder out of an old galvanized tub turned upside down, with a light in the center. When the chicks were small, I put a four-foot-square piece of wood and a piece of old cotton sack over the top to keep the chicks warm. When the chicks got bigger, I removed the canvas and the brooder tub. My older sister Harmeda helped me with the project. Carl was into sports and other things and didn't take much interest in the chicks. He had selected a new hybrid chick and I choose Rhode Island Reds. Well, Carl's chickens were almost twice as big as mine, and he won reserve grand champion at the chicken show. I think I won fifth place. One great thing about the chicken project was that we sure had lots of fried chicken, and later we had some chickens to lay eggs.

In the earlier days, when we butchered, generally my stepfather did the hog killing. (Mom did the chicken killing.) Once the hogs were killed, we hung them up by their back feet and then laid them in a large tub of hot water and scraped the hair off. We never had a freezer so we cured the meat with a salt cure. Mom would cook up the fat for lard and put it in big cans. We ground up the scrap meat, and Mom made sausage and cooked it in the oven and then put it in the lard. It would keep pretty well there for a long time.

**I was about 15 or 16 years old here.
Eleventh grade class president, senior year editor of
the school paper, president of the 4-H Club.**

With six kids, food didn't last very long. We ate lots of oatmeal, potatoes, onions, and gravy and bread; meat was special. We did raise a lot of things to eat, and when the crops were in season, we had plenty. Mom would can lots of cucumbers for pickles, and we would store vegetables in the dugout cellar.

In those days we didn't have indoor plumbing; that meant going to the outhouse or the plum thicket. For night, we had slop jars. With eight people, that outhouse had to be moved and a new hole dug often. I am one that is thankful to the Lord for the indoor plumbing of today.

In the winter the wind really blows hard in western Oklahoma. We called the storms "cold northers." Our place on Eastern Avenue where I lived till I was six did have indoor plumbing. After that until I was nineteen, we had no indoor water or toilets, which made for a cold run in the night. Neither was there any heat except for a wood stove heater. I was a pretty good woodcutter, and I can still cut wood pretty well. The first time I remember sweating in the winter was when I was sawing wood on one end of a six-foot crosscut saw.

Many times we had well problems and had to haul water, mostly in ten-gallon cream cans. When I was just starting to drive, my brother Carl had a 1940 Ford. Once, when he was away on a harvest job, I took the Ford and went for water, maybe three miles down Ladessa Road. On those one-lane dirt roads, passing was tight. I had to pass an oncoming car, and I cut back in too quickly. I grazed the trailer the car was pulling, smashed the left hubcap of Carl's car, and dinged the left front fender. As I recall, I took the right rear hubcap and put it on in place of the one that got smashed. I also worked the fender over a bit, but when you turned fully left, the tire rubbed the fender. Carl soon discovered the problem, and when I was with him and the tire scraped the fender, he would look over at me and say a few choice words. Auto body work might not be one of my gifts.

Carl and I were always trading cars. My first car was a 1940 Chevrolet. I had gone to the salvage yard with my stepdad, and a man came in and said he wanted to sell his car. As I recall, he said he would sell it for forty dollars. I had always been good at saving money and I had forty dollars. My stepdad agreed, and I soon owned a 1940 Chevrolet coupe. I did some minor repairs to it and traded it to Carl for his 1946 International pickup. I painted the pickup green with blue fenders. I recall getting stuck in the sand with it and stripping the rack and pinion (rear end). I learned not to gun the vehicle too hard in the sand; it was best to use a light foot and rock it back and forth. I later traded that pickup for a 1950 Ford. It had an overdrive and was a good car.

I purchased a couple other junk cars and salvaged parts from them. When our crops failed on the farm, we would buy junk cars and sell parts and iron. My job would be to salvage the copper and precious metals. When we started, we didn't have a cutting torch. We would tie a chain to the doors and pull them off with the truck, then cut the body up with an axe.

ACCEPTING CHRIST AS LORD AND SAVIOR

It was fall of the year that I was fifteen, and we were living on the farm on Ladessa Road. My brother Carl and I had been helping our stepdad work on a cotton trailer. He asked us to go get him some smoking tobacco, which we were happy to do. Carl had his first car, a 1935 Ford. We went over to the store, but it was closed. We stood around telling stories with our friends, and then we headed back home.

On the way we had to pass Russell Baptist Church. We knew the preacher's kids; we went to school with them. The church was having a revival, and the meeting was letting out as we passed by. We soon saw a car coming up behind us. It was the preacher's

Kaiser. Joel, the preacher's son, was driving and he waived us down. We stopped and he came over and told us about the revival and about Jesus. Then he asked us if we had ever asked Jesus to be our Savior.

**Russell Baptist Church, which I joined
after accepting Jesus as Savior**

I said yes, but it never seemed to make much difference. He explained it was more than just words. We needed to start coming to church and reading the Bible. It was a commitment to God (Christ Jesus).

Once again I prayed and asked Jesus into my life.

Then he said, "If you really mean it, let's go back to the church and tell the world."

We did, and we went home rejoicing. The next evening we took our stepbrother and stepsisters to church, and they asked Jesus to come into their lives. Our Mom rededicated her life, too.

My stepfather didn't want to become a Christian, but he respected our decision.

Thereafter I started reading my Bible and praying and telling others. It has been over fifty years and I still read my Bible and pray daily and tell others about Jesus.

Burt Day's store with movie house in back.
Russell, Oklahoma.

I was a bit verbal about my faith. Once in science class, the teacher, Mr. Crab, sort of wanted to poke fun at me. He asked me to explain how Noah put all those animals in that boat (ark).

I replied, "Mr. Crab, God could have put all those animals in a fruit jar if He had wanted to." Mr. Crab didn't reply.

In my junior year I sort of had my faith tested. I had some growing to do. One thing I had to do was to clean up my cursing. And one country sport was raiding the neighbors' watermelon patches. Even the boy that led me to Christ was part of the raiding game. We, too, had a patch of melons, but raiding the patches was an acceptable part of being a country boy. We would bust the melon and eat the heart—the best part. On one such trip, we were having a great time raiding a neighbor's patch until we heard what sounded like a shot. We took off running, and I ran into a barbed wire fence. Yes, a few cuts, but that was just part of growing up in watermelon country. We never considered that stealing. But the more I read my Bible the less interested I was in watermelon raids.

ON MY OWN, MAKING MY TOTAL LIVING AND HELPING OTHERS

By the beginning of my junior year in high school, my stepfather had left us, and I had gone out and found a farmer that needed help and had an old house for us to live in.

Mr. Olive was a kind man and I became his hired hand, doing most all his work. He gave us a house to live in, and I worked for him after school and on weekends. Tom Olive was a good man, but a firm boss. He had heart trouble and was unable to do hard work. He carried a pint of whiskey behind his pickup seat and took a shot once in a while for his heart, or so he said.

My starting pay was seventy-five cents an hour. On my first day on the job, he instructed me to drive the 1937 John Deere tractor over to the field where I was to plant cotton. I had only driven a tractor a very little and that was not one that I had driven. To start those old John Deeres, you had to open the two petcocks and turn the big open flywheel till the tractor started and ran a few minutes; then you would turn off the petcocks and close the gas and open the coal oil valve.

I turned the big flywheel and got it going. Then I headed to the field where I was to plant cotton. Mr. Olive was there waiting, sitting on the edge of a low trailer with the seeds in it. I pulled the John Deere up behind it and pulled the big lever that acted as the clutch and brake. Well, that didn't stop the tractor in time! The front wheel jumped into the trailer that Mr. Olive was sitting on. Well, heart trouble or no, he flew out of the trailer! You talk about apologizing!

Well, Tom Olive was a truly kind man. He said, "Back it out," which I did. Then he gave me instructions on tractor driving. One thing he pointed out was that I should line up my sight with a telephone post or fence post and drive as straight as I could toward it. I soon learned how to come out to the end of the row and hit my wheel brake and turn that Deere around and head back down the next row without missing a beat.

Many times I would eat lunch at the Ladessa store; the Olive farm was just down the road. Les, the owner of the store, told me one day that Tom had told him he would have fired me for the tractor-in-the-trailer episode, but he knew I was trying and he kept me.

For two years I was Mr. Olive's man, raising some fine crops of cotton, maize and wheat. Mr. Olive also had a Ford tractor that I used to cultivate the crops with. I truly enjoyed the farm work. I had a jungle hat which I wore, and I recall seeing my rich friends going to town to play and swim as I drove those tractors at seventy-five cents an hour.

I also worked for Mr. Cowan, who raised sheep as well as farm crops. It was during that time that I raised some Duroc pigs. One of them died and I felt bad, but I never knew why it died. The other pig did fine, and I took him to the fair.

I have been good with saving and managing my money most all of my life. I opened a bank account at Mangum and had a checking account in high school.

The school principal liked me, and he knew I was working hard and providing a house for my mom and two other children.

The bus-driving jobs generally went to seniors at our little school. (There were about two hundred students in the whole school, ten in our class at grade 12.) In the summer of my junior year, Mr. Ross told me to go to bus-driving school and he would give me a job, even though I was just a junior.

The bank in Mangum where I had my first bank account

I went for a week at the college in Weatherford. I did fine all week, making good grades, but for my driving test, I was driving a new Chevrolet with booster brakes. The buses I had driven at school were old Fords and you had to almost stand on the breaks to stop them, Well, I went a bit too fast in a school zone and my stopping was not to his liking, so he failed me.

I was not happy to go home like a dog with his tail between his legs, but I never complained. One of my good friends got the job, a senior, and somehow God still met all my needs, which he still does—very well.

The next year I was a senior and I had my chauffeur's license and I got a bus-driving job. I recall once I got the bus stuck in the snow and Mr. Ross just happened to come by. He went to a nearby farm and borrowed a big John Deere tractor. He hooked it on the bus bumper, which he pulled off. I tied the bumper back on and the next day I took it to the shop for repair. Mr. and Mrs. Ross were special people that God seemed to give a message to, saying, "This is one of My boys. Take good care of him."

MULES AND HORSES

When we moved to the ten acres, our stepfather brought a donkey home for us kids. We piled on his back, and we made a cart for him to pull us around in. We had great fun with Jack! I recall once he was pulling us down the road in the cart and he saw or smelled a mare in the field. Well, Jack went over to see the mare, and when he went into the bar ditch, the cart almost turned over.

I've already told about my first horse getting repossessed for his feed. Well, when we lived on Ladessa road, we worked for an older gentleman, Elmo Hurst. He had an old cutting horse named Pacos. He took a liking to Jim and me and gave the horse to us, asking my stepdad to keep him till he died. We really enjoyed Pacos. He was a great horse.

My brother Carl got a horse named Trixie. She was very pretty, but not good natured; she would almost go sideways in her gait.

We sometimes went down to the North Fork of the Red River, which was behind our place, and played cowboy. We could spread the barbed wires, and old Pacos would hunker down and go through. Well, one fall one of those rain and hail storms came and wiped out our crops, and our stepdad sold old Pacos. Jim and I hated to see him go, but without money or feed, we understood.

GIRLS

My first girlfriend was when I was in the third or fourth grade—
Patsy Jo. She would come by my desk and kick me or something.
Some romance!

Then in high school there was Betty Sue. My buddy Gerald
stole her, sitting by her on the bus. Then there was Betty Nell
and her sister. I sat by them at the ballgame once or twice. Then
in high school I went with Darlene and Bertha, and then there
was a girl that came with her family to Mangum to pull cotton.

After high school, I went on the wheat harvest and met a girl
on a trip to town. More details on that later.

In California, there were several girls, but then I met my
Nancy Rae and since then there have been no other girls.

THE WHEAT HARVEST

Young men in Western Oklahoma looked forward to going on
the wheat harvest, generally from Texas to North Dakota. Carl
had gone, and when I finished high school, I made a deal to drive
a truck on the wheat harvest. I told my old boss, Mr. Olive, and
he understood.

This was sort of like the old cattle drives. We cut wheat and I
hauled it to the elevator. I took my army cot and a bag of clothes.
My boss, Mr. Griffin, drove his pickup.

It was a small crew—two trucks, and two combines. We pulled
the combines on big trailers; my truck was a REO. Those combines
were sixteen feet wide and we drove like most young men—too fast.
When our caravan came down the road, we got plenty of respect.
Once when we stopped, I had lost a boomer and stopped just in time.

One fond memory was in Nebraska, near Carnie. It started
raining, and when it rained, we could not cut wheat. We slept in

the barn when it rained and other times under the stars. Much of my growing-up years I slept outside under the stars in the summer. I still love the open spaces and the sky.

Donny, the other truck driver, and I played pool in the loft of the farmer's barn and hitchhiked to Carnie. One of the things I saw in Carnie was a city park that was like nothing I had ever seen. It had little bridges and paths; it was a showplace.

On one of those trips to town, Donny and I were walking around the square and the locals came by. They needed another man for their extra girl and they called out to me, "You with the straw hat, want to go to a dance?" I was happy to do that. I was not too good at dancing, but I had a great time. I can't recall if I got to kiss the girl or not, but it was a fun evening.

In those days, young people would often walk around the square, and the ones with cars would drive around the square. I guess maybe that's why they made squares in those small towns?

As the rain continued, Mr. Griffin came to me and said he couldn't afford to keep paying me the $2.25 per hour, which was big money in those days. He was paying me by the day. I was the only one that had a cot to sleep on, and I told Mr. Griffin he could use it and I would take the bus back to Mangum. Well, before we got to the bus station, Mr. Griffin decided he could afford me after all, and I stayed to the end and drove the rig back home to Mangum.

THE FORT SILL JOB, WORKING FOR MR. HUGHEY

When I graduated from Centralvue, I planned to go to college, but one of the boys in my class asked me to come and work with him and his dad, who was an electrical contractor at Fort Sill Army Base. They treated me like family. We rented a small apartment in nearby Lawton and I was an electrical helper.

I had been building things on the farm, once taking an old refrigerator compressor and turning it into an air compressor and battery charger. Learning to do electrical work was of great interest to me.

I was the low man on the team, and when no one wanted to go under the house because there was talk of a rattlesnake under the church next door, I was the man. I recall saying the Twenty-third Psalm as I crawled down those low ditches putting in the pipe and wires.

Once Curtis and I had installed a lot of switches and Curtis Sr. came and told us they were all upside down. So we learned to install them the correct way.

I really enjoyed the electrical work. I went to college at night and took some basic courses. I recall mentioning Jesus in an essay paper and the teacher gave me a very low grade on it. It seems the anti-God movement had started in the schools.

I was never a big party person and never drank very much. Oklahoma was dry in those days except for 3.2% beer (low-alcohol beer) and what one could buy at the bootleggers'. My buddy and I would go to a dance or movie, and I often had to drive. I knew I had committed my life to Christ and I never wanted to make a fool of myself or dishonor Christ.

We finished our contract about Christmas of 1956, and Curtis and I set out to find more electrical work. One story I recall was that we had a hickey (pipe bender) missing. A lady came by with her child, pulling a wagon. I asked her if they had seen the tool, and she replied, "No." Then the boy spoke up, "Mom, is that what you told me to put in the wagon yesterday?" She looked a bit sheepish and went on.

Chapter 2

The Years after Leaving Home

MY TRIP FROM MANGUM TO LOS ANGELES

(From my diary)

Sunday, January 6, 1957

Curtis Jr. and I set out for Borger, Texas, about 10:00 a.m. Curtis took the lead in his 1951 Studebaker. I wouldn't push my 1952 Mercury as hard as he would his Studebaker, so I lost sight of him after he turned west from Reed. I met him again at his uncle Lee Hughey's at Wellington. The next time I saw him was at White Deer, Texas. He said the highway patrol stopped him before he got there. At Skellytown, we called Wade Hood, a friend of the Hugheys, and went to the main highway to wait for his boy to come and take us to their place. We waited at Skellytown and the boy waited at Borger. So we missed him.

Curtis and I went on to Borger. At Borger I stopped for gas and Curtis lost me again. I called Wade Hood's wife and she told me to wait at the 66 Station in the nearby town of Phillips. I met Wade there, and he and I went and found Curtis. He was still looking for Wade's house.

Wade had a nice family of four children—two nearly grown boys, a girl about 16, and a small girl. The Hoods told us what we could find in Borger, and Curtis and I went to Borger and rented a small apartment for a week.

Monday, January 7, 1957

The next day we went from place to place trying to get a job. We finally decided that we couldn't find work in Borger, not for a week at least, so we got $8 of our $12 rent back and set out for Dumas, Texas. We went to the show that night at Dumas. The movie was "Hollywood or Bust," starring Dean Martin and Jerry Lewis. It was a great picture. Then Curtis and I rented us a $2.50 room at the Plains Hotel.

Tuesday, January 8, 1957

The next morning Curtis and I set out early to find a job. We tried everything around there. We were too young, didn't have experience, hadn't been in the service, or something. From there we went back to Borger. We went back by Wade's house and thanked them for the help they had given us. Then we set out for Amarillo, Texas. Curtis lost me again and we met late that evening at the electricians union office. We went downtown and rented a $2.50 room at the Ross Hotel. We went skating that night. I had a lot of fun.

Wednesday, January 9, 1957

We set out early to find work in Amarillo. At 10 a.m. we were both discouraged and Curtis and I said goodbye. He set out for home and I set out for California.

I filled up my Mercury with gas and set out on Route 66. A terrible dust storm was just beginning. I drove about five miles and picked up a hitchhiker. He was a poor broke fellow setting out for California with fifty-eight cents in his pocket; anyway that's what he told me. I couldn't tell him to get out, and yet I couldn't eat and let him do without...

The dust storm got worse and worse until you couldn't see the white line on the road. We pulled off for a while, and then another driver got brave and passed us with his lights on, and I followed him. As we got over into New Mexico, we began to hit some mountains and the dust diminished.

I drove through New Mexico and to Holbrook, Arizona, and then I let him drive, even though he didn't have a license. I was tired and sleepy and I dozed off to sleep, and when I woke up, we were in a great national forest in Arizona. It was about 1:30 in the morning and the rain was pouring down.

He drove a few miles further, and I took over the driving again. We soon came out of the forest and went up into the mountains. The roads were narrow, winding, and steep, and some had no railing. I drove in the mountains for about thirty miles before we came to a store where they had to generate their own electricity. I bought some gas there for thirty-five cents a gallon and we set out again. I drove till about 2:40 a.m. Then I pulled off of the road near the top of a mountain and we slept till morning. This was a very interesting day of my life.

Thursday, January 10, 1957

When we woke up it was raining. I started the motor, but the transmission would not take hold and the car would not move. We tried to push the car back onto the road so we could let it roll down the mountain, but the ground was too soft for us to move it, so we waited for a push. A few cars come by but they didn't stop. Finally a state truck came by and pulled us back onto the road and we rolled down the mountain. I thought that if the car got to rolling, it would kick into gear, but it didn't. I let it roll as far as it would. Then I again got out and tried to adjust the transmission, but it was in vain. A few more cars came by, but they wouldn't push us. Finally another fellow in a state pickup came by and pushed us up to the top of another mountain. We again rolled down as far as we could and waited for another push. Several cars passed us, and then a fellow came along in a company car and pushed us to the place where the state kept their road equipment, then he went on. There was a house there, so I went down to see if I could get some oil for the transmission. The hitchhiker stayed at the car.

There was only a lady at the house and she didn't know of any oil. She said I might find some in the power shed. I looked, but there were only empty cans. When I came back around the house, there was a car up beside mine. It came down to where I was, and it turned out that the driver was the head of the highway crew. He got me three quarts of oil and wouldn't take any pay for it. He took me back up to my car and I poured the oil into the transmission. It took hold like new! I was a very happy boy, and the hitchhiker was in better spirits too.

We started on toward Phoenix, Arizona. We left the mountains and hit the desert. When we reached the edge of Phoenix, I saw orchards of oranges, lemons, grapefruit, grapes and tall palm trees. I pulled over and when I stopped the car, I saw a flat tire on the rear of my car. We fixed the flat in the rain and went on into Phoenix. There I bought us some hamburgers. We went to the employment office in Phoenix and learned there was nothing available around there. We looked around and I bought a tire for five dollars. I thought it was a buy even though it was a black wall and really too small for my car. We mounted it at a Whiting Brothers station. I used Whiting Brothers gas because they gave me a discount card. I got 1 cent off each gallon.

At a place about four hours' drive from Phoenix, I stopped for gas and my car wouldn't start. I put my razor and shaving cream in my pocket and went into the restroom and shaved with ice cold water. It was worth it to have a clean shave.

There was a young man at the station trying to get a ride. He saw me working on the car and he came over and tried to help us. He got the station man to push us, and I gave him a ride to the place he was going. After I let him out, we stopped and had some coffee. The car again failed to start, so I set the timing and it kicked right off. Again I felt good because my car ran better.

We entered the state of California late that night. I again let the hitchhiker drive. About 1:00 a.m. we stopped at Desert Center, a station and café in the middle of the desert, and slept. The hitchhiker slept in the front seat and I slept in the back.

Friday, January 11, 1957

The next morning we rose early and set out for Los Angeles. We arrived about the middle of the day.

The hitchhiker, who said his name was Joe Thomason and who said he was a cook, had left Amarillo with fifty-eight cents. The night before we arrived in Los Angeles, he wired a friend for ten dollars. He was supposed to pick it up at the Western Union on his arrival. When we reached the main part of town, I asked him if he could find the Western Union office and he said he could. So I said so long, and he thanked me for the ride and grub, and I drove on. Later in the day I rented a room at Hotel Richard, where I am at the present time.

I left Mangum with about a hundred dollars, and left Amarillo with about eighty dollars. I arrived with about thirty dollars, and that is the story of my trip to Los Angeles, California.

Joe (Donald A. Nordine)

P. S.

Tuesday, January 29, 1957

Today I did my first day's work for the Pacific Telephone Co. I am an installer. The fellow I worked with today, and probably will in the near future, is Mr. Hummell. He is from Iowa, and seems like a nice man to work with, but I must say he works fast and hard. The bag of empty telephone boxes in the front of his truck was the fullest of any I saw.

I ate dinner at a café, or should I say I ordered a bowl of chili that I couldn't eat. I cashed my last twenty that I have here tonight to pay my room rent, which is $1.25 a day. Even though it looks as if I may run low on money before I get paid on February 15, June and Art told me not to go hungry. (June runs the diner and Art runs the hotel.) When I received my mail at the hotel desk, I got my balance from the City National Bank of Lawton, Oklahoma. My balance was $47.09.

I have just done a small washing and gathered up what I shall take to the laundry. Now I will read a few chapters in the Bible and go to bed.

This has been the day of Donald Nordine, January 29, 1957.

Donald Nordine (Joe)

Friday, February 1, 1957

I have just completed my first week's work for Pacific Telephone Company.

D.A. Nordine

TEMPLE BAPTIST CHURCH

Soon after I landed in Los Angeles, I saw the big sign for Temple Baptist Church. I was a member of Russell Baptist Church and so I attended Temple and enjoyed it. They had a great youth group and Dr. Harnish was a fine speaker. I recall once George Beverly Shea was there, and Ralph Carmichael was the music director. It was in the Philharmonic Auditorium.

I was a green country boy and a sweet girl, Ruth, took a liking to me. I drove her new Oldsmobile up to a church camp for the young people. They were ready for me. "As soon as it's pitch dark," someone said, "we are going snipe hunting." Surely a country boy would know what snipe hunting was! I played along as if I knew.

Well, they convinced me to hold a gunny sack. They were to go and chase the snipes to me and I was to catch them and bring them back. How dumb can you be?? First they made lots of noise and then it got quiet. Well, after what seemed like a long time, I finally went back to the cabin. Oh, did they laugh, asking me how many snipes I caught!

I never knew if the girl, Ruth, was in on the prank. She soon found another fellow and they married. I never asked him how he was at snipe hunting.

THE ROOMING HOUSE

After I stayed in the cheap hotel for a few weeks, my working friend, Harlo, told me about a rooming house in Huntington Park. It was on Alburtis, and I had a nice room on the second floor. It cost twenty-one dollars a week, including supper and a bag lunch. The meal arrangement pleased me, as I never was much for cooking.

I recall the old Mercury was still leaking transmission oil, and I finally parked with the right wheel on the curb, crawled under the car, and took out the transmission. I purchased a replacement at the salvage yard and put it in, using a low milk crate to slide it in. I had started going to East Los Angeles College at nights, and the transmission I installed lasted only a few miles before the torque converter broke. I had to make another trip to the salvage yard. As I recall, my salvage transmission cost forty dollars. That time it lasted till I traded the car for a beautiful Silver Hawk made by Studebaker.

I worked for the Bell Phone company for a few months and then one of the men at the boarding house told me about a job at the Purex Corporation soap and bleach factory. It paid a little more, so I quit the phone company and went to work for the Purex Corporation.

After living on Alburtis for maybe a year, I moved to another boarding house, which was run by Mrs. Mack, a great cook. While living at the boarding houses, I made several friends, one of whom was Warren Toby.

On one outing, Toby and I went out to the hills and desert with a man named Hudson. After we had walked for a time, Hudson said to Toby, "How are you doing?" It seemed a bit odd to me that he would ask him how he was doing, but then Hudson turned to me and said, "Toby has a glass leg and foot." I had noticed he had a slight limp. He lifted his pants leg and sure enough he had a glass leg. I said, "Toby, let me carry that rifle."

Well, Toby and I became friends. That was in 1957. He worked in a steel mill and was from South Texas. One time he went to Mexico and as he was coming back from Ensenada, he went to sleep and ran over some roadside rails. They banged his oil pan into his rods. I took him down there a couple of times. We put a pan on the motor, did some minor body work, and paid his fines to two or three people. We got the car released and he drove it back.

In early 1959 Toby and I went to a Cliffie Stone TV show. They had a dance floor and I met my future wife and in-laws, first dancing with Nancy's sister and then with Nancy. We were married a few weeks later on February 14, 1959.

My grandfather Brown

My grandmother Brown

Nancy's parents, Howard and Stella Fennell, with Nancy and I

My sisters Fredia and Harmeda with our mom and I

A family gathering at my sister's home

Four brothers: Burl, me, Ollie, and Elbert

Sons Vance and Kevin about 1965

A fishing day with friend Vern Hollinger

Our family around 1982: Vance, Kevin, Don and Nancy

Vance and Gloria's wedding day

Gloria with Wesley, Vance, Mary, me, Nancy, and Rose

**Granddaughters Rose and Mary at our home.
The cactus behind them blooms only once every ten years.**

Howard and Stella at our home celebrating their fiftieth anniversary

My older brother Ollie and me at Ollie's home

My granddaughter, Mary Grace Nordine, and me

My grandchildren, Rose, Wes and Mary, with me at Mt. San Jacinto

Son Kevin building our La Habra Heights house

Kevin helping build our house

Our La Habra Heights home finished

**Missionary friends, the Grieners, at our home
with our granddaughter Mary**

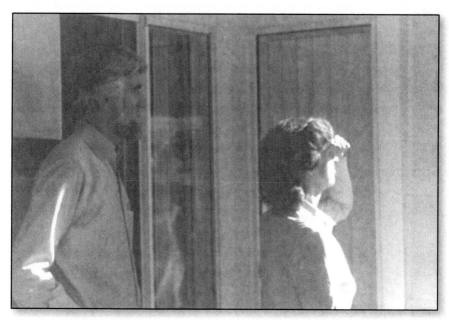

Missionary friends Louis and Connie Van Ness in our home

My sister Harmeda and I at the house I bought for our
mother in Oklahoma City. October 2004

Nancy and me on our trip to the Holy Land

On a trip to Arizona

On a land inspection tour

On an Alaska cruise

My salmon and the boat captain at
the Cedars Alaskan Fishing Lodge

Nancy and me on a trip in Oklahoma

At a family gathering in Oklahoma City

On a horse ride by Big Bear Lake, CA

Chapter 3

The Years after Marrying Nancy

MARRIED AND WORKING

Before I met Nancy, one of the older men at Purex gave me some advice about choosing a wife. He said, "Take a look at the girl's mother, because that is most likely what your wife will look like in twenty or thirty years." Well, Nancy's mom was a nice-looking lady and her dad, at six foot three and a half, was a great-looking guy. I recall he was in the sheriff reserves, and I came in and saw him in his uniform. He looked very impressive.

Nancy and I were married at Bell Baptist Church. Rev. King did the service. I had a couple of men from my boarding house attend, and Nancy had a couple of ladies from her work, in addition to her Mom, Dad, and sister, Sally. I gave the preacher ten dollars for doing the service.

We had rented a small apartment on Loveland Street in Bell Garden. I had under a hundred dollars and Nancy had about three hundred dollars in the bank. I owned a 1955 Chevrolet clear and one shotgun and a rifle, which I hocked for some extra cash. All my courting had taken its toll on my finances. I was working at Purex, and Nancy was working at Prudential Overall Supply.

For over fifty years we have had a great relationship. I have often repeated the advice the man at Purex gave me.

Our wedding day

Nancy and our 1955 Chevrolet

I was doing okay at the Purex job, but it was hard on my health. Bleach and soap plants are possibly the reason I developed hay fever. One of my bosses at Purex was Frank Buel. He was a nice boss and treated me okay. He would often come to our work area and rub his hands together and say, "I have a little job for you." One of the nasty jobs there was dumping soap.

Once our production line broke, and we went out to repair pallets to keep busy. We were betting on how many hits it took to drive a nail. Frank was watching us and he came out and said, "Men, I want to hear those hammers going ratta-tat-tat."

I broke my left hand there. I was working on what we called the hand trend line and the soap had spilled on the floor. I picked up a five-gallon jug of soap and slipped and fell on the jug, and it broke a couple of bones in my hand. I drove myself to the doctor and was back on the job the next day.

Our wedding cake and kiss in our first apartment

After we got married, I didn't keep in touch with my old boarding house buddies. I was too busy with my new wife, and then in June of 1959 the Army drafted me. I had not notified them of my California address till after I was married. I knew that the draft board in Mangum would put the men who moved out of the area at the top of the list. I felt that being married, I was safe, but I was wrong.

When I was drafted into the army, Purex paid me a small salary; I think it was twenty dollars a month. That meant I had a job when I got out.

U.S. ARMY

I got my greeting to report for my army physical in Los Angeles. On June 14, 1959, my fellow recruits and I traveled by train first class to Fort Ord, which is near the beach. We were barracked in the newer three-story block buildings. The training was tough. I never knew I could get sore in so many places. We did rifle training on the beach about two miles from the barracks, and they would run us till several men would fall down and couldn't run any more. Then we would get a break. Someone had told me to not be the first or the last, and as I recall I never fell out. I kept my nose clean and did my job.

Nancy sent me a box of peaches from her dad's tree, and one morning when we were standing in formation for mail call, the sergeant called, "Nordine, there is a package for you in the mail room. Take a mop." The peaches had leaked all over the place. I wrote Nancy, "Thanks, but please no more peaches."

The discipline was pretty hard. One soldier shaved his head. That was before shaved heads were popular, and he got in trouble and was given KP duty. Another soldier, Knott, had also shaved his head, but he got some black shoe polish and covered his bald head and he didn't get disciplined for it.

Knott was a prankster, and one day some of the men stuffed

him in a trash can and put it in the mop closet. I came by and he was kicking the door. He was stuck and could not free himself. I had mercy on him and pulled him free.

After six weeks of basic training, as I recall, we had an open house for family. I was on a team to display taking an M1 rifle in the standing position, field stripping it, putting it back together, and coming back to attention position. I came in second place. I had borrowed some parts from my friend's loose-fitting rifle and that really helped. Nancy came up and we went to town and had a remarkable weekend.

After finishing my basic training, I was given leave and then orders to report to Fort Lewis, Washington. This time I went by regular bus. I recall playing cards with a little girl who taught me the game of Hearts. I am not sure if I have ever played it since. At Fort Lewis, I was assigned to an infantry company. I had an MOS (military occupation specialty, or job description) for heavy equipment operator, as I had experience in tractor and truck driving. So much for my MOS! I was a rifleman in the infantry.

In that part of Washington it rains about eight or nine months of the year, and that is when they play war. I am thankful we didn't have a real war going at that time. I, being a Christian, didn't believe in killing. Shooting blanks was fun, but I did not and still do not think war is an answer.

I felt I was a pretty good poker player, and we had a good deal of spare time, but it didn't take long for me to learn I wasn't very good. An old-timer watched us new men playing, quarter limit, and asked to come in. We agreed, and he soon had the pot.

After a few weeks of playing war games in the forest in the rain, we were on a break. The captain came up to me and asked how it was going. Captain Gilkey was an okay captain. He asked about my family, and I mentioned that I would sure like to go get my wife. He asked when and I said, "This weekend." He said, "Okay."

For a soldier to leave the base, he needed a signed pass. Well, on Friday I went down to the clerk's office and found that no pass had been signed. I was a little fearful of the office, as the first sergeant had chewed me out for not saying "Sir" every time I spoke to the captain. Saturday came, and still no signed pass. Sunday I went to chapel. I saw the captain there. I greeted him and asked about my pass. "Oh," he said, "I'll come by and sign it this afternoon." I kept watching for the captain's car. Well, finally the clerk called me and said my pass was signed. I had been watching for the captain's car, but I later learned that the captain had called and the clerk had signed the pass for the captain.

I went over to McChord Field and caught a hop. If the military has a plane and an empty seat, they let a soldier ride free. Well, the first plane was an old prop job and one engine caught fire just as we were taking off. It turned out not to be too bad, and we returned and took another plane to Los Angeles, or most of the way. We finished the trip on the bus. Once in Bell Gardens, I had to work fast, as I had to report back to Fort Lewis by Thursday. In the Army, a three-day pass generally allows for a day of grace, so I had until Thursday. I recall that as I was driving back with Nancy, we stopped to look at some sights and, of course, do a little smooching. When we tried to open the car door to get back in, it was locked. I had no tools and I finally had to break the little wing window to get in. Those 1955 Chevrolets were nice-looking cars, but they were short on quality.

In Washington, we rented a little room and a half behind a burger stand. Nancy was learning to cook. Once she put a can of green beans in the oven without opening it. The kitchen was just a little alcove off the other room. We were in the bedroom/living room and we heard an explosion. Nancy commented that the artillery for the maneuvers was sure getting close. We had green beans all over the place!

We later moved up into a one-bedroom house in a trailer court. Thirty years later, in 1990, we visited Canada and the Northwest and went by that little house, which was made of sheets of pressed wood. It was still there and looked about the same.

We generally went to church in Olympia. We didn't develop many friends at that little church, but my memory of it is okay. Nancy took a job at the capital doing keypunch. We were living there when we had our first child, Vance.

That year our battle group was the enemy for the division, and we played big war games at Yakima, in the dry part of the state. My new marching boots made my heel sore, and I went to the doctor. They put me on low quarters, and I did detail labor as needed around the building till I was better. Then one day while we were out playing war, my squad leader, Sergeant Boyd, came up to me and said, "Nordine, I heard you're going to be the new armor and supply clerk." Sergeant Jackson, the supply sergeant, asked that I be picked for the job. He seemed to like my work on the detail days while working for him.

So they sent me to arms mechanic school. I have always had a business mind and the job was a good fit. I am a natural mechanic. I would go get and sign for supplies, manage the weapons of our company, repair them, and keep them in good order. I inspected the weapons of all the troops in our company. It was protocol for the armor clerk to clean the weapons of the captain and first sergeant. Everyone else cleaned their own.

I had time to do some sewing on the side. I learned to sew on the farm on a Singer pedal sewing machine, helping my mother turn over the cotton sacks we used for pulling the cotton. We would wear one side out, then turn them over and wear the other side out, and then change ends. These were ten- or twelve-foot-long bags. Now in the army, I was the company tailor. When soldiers got promoted, they needed new stripes sewed on their uniforms. I charged ten cents a stripe. One month I made an extra forty dollars sewing. That was pretty good, as my salary was only about a hundred dollars. It varied if I got extra for housing, as I lived off post. I went to work, like a job.

My sergeant, Jackson, was an older man and a fine Christian. We got along like father and son. He was very careful to keep everything in good safe order. I often hauled the laundry down post and picked up the clean laundry. Once when we were changing captains, we took inventory and we were short forty pillowcases. Sergeant Jackson was upset and didn't know what to do. He didn't want to have a shortage. I went up to the mess hall. I got along good with the mess sergeant. He got bundles of white rags for cleaning, which were really old sheets. I told him what I needed, and he gave me a bundle of rags. That night I made forty pillowcases. Sergeant Jackson was a happy man, and I made Specialist 4 in only fourteen months.

**Spec 4 Hickman and Spec 4 Nordine cleaning shovels
at field exercises in Yakima, Washington**

Back to playing the enemy in Yakima, we flew in on airplanes about the size of a B29, but they were special planes. They carried a three-quarter-ton truck and a squad of men. We sat on wooden benches on each side. We landed in the open field. The plane didn't fully stop. The door in the rear dropped down, the truck rolled off, and we ran out after it. A jet came over and shot at us, and we tried to hide and shoot back (blanks). It was fun, but please, no live ammo. I came down sick and went on sick call to the tent hospital. Nancy was in the hospital having our first child, Vance Aaron. Our company commander came and told me that if I was well enough, I could hop a ride back to Madigan, the army hospital. Nancy soon quit working outside the home and stayed home to take care of our son.

The company had gripe meetings once in a while, and the men could complain or speak their mind about difficulties. One of the platoon sergeants said "Nordine is an S.O.B. in the arms inspections." The men came and told me, and I asked the first sergeant to call the platoon sergeant in. His defense was, "Nordine is tough." The first sergeant came and told me that he was paying me a backhanded compliment, that I was doing a good job. I had rebuilt my arms racks and my sergeant was very pleased with my work.

Lots of men would go to town and spend their pay and then mooch money till payday. The first sergeant had an off-limits room where we kept stuff we wanted to be out of sight—extra weapons, etc. It was said that the cook had gotten into trouble and the first sergeant had bailed him out. Well, on payday, the cook ran a special poker game in that room, putting 10 percent in a kitty for the first sergeant.

A person could make a few dollars loaning money and lose some when soldiers went AWOL or just refused to pay, as the Army frowned on loaning money. Generally you loaned ten dollars and expected to get fifteen or twenty dollars back on payday. I wonder how it is today.

I completed my active Army duty in June 1961, transitioning to the Reserves until 1965.

RETURNING TO SOUTHERN CALIFORNIA

Nancy and I both liked the cooler Northwest, but Purex was keeping a job open for me, so when my time was up, we returned to Downey. I purchased a little two-wheeled trailer and pulled it behind our 1955 Chevrolet. We stayed a few weeks with Nancy's folks, the Fennells, till we rented an apartment in South Gate, near Purex. We developed a few friends on Burke Avenue that we still know today, including Sam and Glenna Holloway.

We joined the Baptist Church and enjoyed the young peoples' class and fellowship. Dr. Kopp was the main pastor.

When I returned to Purex I had about four years' seniority. We would bid on job openings, so that gave me some breaks. I started attending Cerritos College and took some classes in welding and related subjects. I was hoping to get into the electrical or maintenance department at Purex.

BUYING OUR FIRST HOME AND DEVELOPING NEW GOALS

After a year or so back at Purex, we decided to buy our first house. One of my old Purex friends was now selling real estate, so I paid him a visit. Eddie was a very intelligent man. He was from Egypt and spoke several languages.

We purchased a home on Dunrobin Avenue in South Downey. It had a big yard. Nancy was now pregnant with our second child, Kevin. We paid about $12,950 for the house, taking over an existing FHA loan, and the owner carried a second mortgage for $1000 at 10 percent. Our payment was $99 per month, and it seemed the lender was overcharging us for some insurance, so we went to Los Angeles and got it straightened out. The man that helped us, Mr. Carr, later became a loan broker whom we worked with.

I had lots of work to do on that property. The prior owner had built a lean-to washhouse and closed in the carport. It was a mess. I restored the house pretty much to what it had been when it was originally built. While taking off some of the old boards, I fell backwards and landed on a nail. Oh, did I have a sore bottom. We picked a pink color to paint the house, but it was too bright and we later changed it.

I was working in the rear yard when the radio announced that President Kennedy had been shot. This was after I went to work in real estate for my old friend Eddie Makasjian and read

William Nickerson's book, *How I Turned $1000 into a Million in Real Estate in My Spare Time*, and Napolean Hill's book, *Think and Grow Rich*.

I first got my real estate license in 1964, and I went to work for Ed Makasjian part time for a year. I worked swing shift at Purex, and I worked real estate from 9 a.m. to 2 p.m. I started reading lots of sales and self-improvement books. Some people from the poor community don't see how to become rich or build wealth; I was one of those people. I had been a hard worker and saver and so was Nancy, but like most people in that status, I could only see a house and a car as the end of the dream. Well, I had some mind work to do. I was also watching Eddie put together some remarkable deals.

While working for Eddie, I even learned to tie a square knot tie. Ed had some ties on the rack, and I took one down and took it apart and retied it till I mastered it. Eddie knew how to make a deal and I soon learned some tricks of the trade. Once you get rolling, people who want to buy a house come looking for you.

I soon made a financial plan for my life. While still at Purex, I listened to my friend and leader Darrell. He told me how he had made a lot of money on Purex stock. Well, I went to the credit union and borrowed $1000 and started purchasing Purex stock. I paid it back from my overtime work. Generally I made about $25 for overtime, and that is about what one share of Purex stock went for at that time. Before I quit Purex, I had ninety shares of stock. I never did as well as Darrell, but I did okay, and it gave me a goal to work toward. This was about 1962 to 1965.

The last year I was at Purex, I was a machine operator making plastic bottles. I was fairly good at it. It was a very dangerous job. One of my fellow operators reached into the big brass bottle molds to retrieve some plastic and got his hand crushed in the mold.

I often worked a double shift, from 3 p.m. to 8 the next

morning. On one of those days, it was almost 8:00 and the day foreman, Mac, came over and made an adjustment on my machine. I told him to keep his hands off my machine till his shift began. He just turned and walked away. I was a little sharp, just finishing my sixteen-hour double shift. Mac was an okay man and foreman, and he didn't let my comment upset him. When he was running the graveyard shift, he drove a little Honda. Foreman Rice had a full-size pickup, and once some of the men went out to the parking lot early and put Mac's little Honda into the back of Rice's pickup.

STARTING TO WORK IN REAL ESTATE

In 1964, when I started working part time in real estate, Eddie, my boss, purchased me a thousand business cards and told me to go door to door, asking people if they wanted to buy or sell real estate.

Well, I started out. I went up my first walk and rang the doorbell. An elderly lady came to the door and I asked those famous words, "Would you like to sell your house?" There was no need to ask if she'd like to buy one. She was obviously too old to be interested buying anything.

To my surprise, she invited me in. Her name was Mrs. Friday, and she was thinking of selling, not then, but a little later. I am not sure, but as I recall, she wanted to move in with a daughter. She mentioned her toilet was running, so I did a minor adjustment for her. I took note of her name, etc., and would go by and see her now and then. One day she listed the house with me—my first doorbell and my first listing! Eddie soon sold the house for her, and when the sale closed, I purchased a high back chair from her. I still have that chair.

In my early days canvassing Eucalyptus Street, I decided to

learn to spell it and I still have it down pat. I rang one doorbell and the lady came to the door. She said she didn't want to sell the house, but her lot was large enough to split, and she wanted to sell part of it. If I would do the paperwork, she would list it with me. Splitting a lot is very time-consuming, but I did it, and Eddie sold the lot for $8000, which was a good price in those days.

On one of my canvassing days, I talked to a lady who wanted to buy a house, so I set out to show property to her and her husband. Mr. Steel was a retired veteran. I finally found a home they liked and wrote up the offer. The house was vacant, and the owner lived in Orange in a newer home. I recall sitting on the couch and smelling dog potty. I looked at my shoe, excused myself, and went out into the yard to clean up. We got the deal together, but I forgot to ask for a termite report. The other broker was a nice man. When I told him of my mistake, he said, "That's okay. FHA always asks for a termite report and requires the seller to pay for it." I think this was my first sale and it went okay. I kept a list of all my buyers and would stop by and see them or send them a newsletter or card. Forty years later, I still have people dropping in. Some years ago I gave that list of buyers to my son Vance, who took over the business.

I enjoyed going on caravan. This was when a bunch of brokers got together and showed each other the houses they had for sale. Once in a while brokers served refreshments and sometimes lunch. I got to know some of the lady brokers by the dishes they fixed, more than the deals we had together. On my open houses, I generally only served minor refreshments. In the early days, we hired a bus to caravan the homes, sometimes cars.

I soon sold a few houses to friends at Purex. One was to a fellow machine operator. While I was working as a machine operator making plastic bottles, I generally ran four machines. The other operators and I rotated machines and watched and helped each other. Marvin was one of that group, and we got along fine. But Marvin's language was very foul, and he often cursed me in a joking way. I felt his comments to me were not acceptable, and I told him I was a Christian. He took it hard and said he wouldn't talk to me, and he didn't for some time. Then one day he came over and apologized. He started going to church and got his life back in tune with God. Later when I was in the real estate business, he called on me to be his agent.

One who surprised me was Mac, the foreman. When I turned in my notice of resignation, Mac called me into his office and asked me to find a larger home for his family. Well, I showed his wife lots of houses, but they saw one for sale by owner and called and told me they were buying that one. They were great folks; they were Catholic Christians with five boys. A few years later, Mac called me up and said, "Don, come over and list our house. Purex has made me a plant manager back east, and they are paying the commission for selling our house." Well, I was most happy to list their house. By this time I had set up a line of credit with my bank, the National Bank of Whittier. The market was slow and I held open houses for Mac and ran ads, but had no takers. Then one day, Mac called me and said, "Don, one of our friends would like to buy our house, but they need to sell their house first. Come over." Being the risk taker that I am, I said, "No problem. If their house doesn't sell in sixty days, I will buy it." I did sell their house, and they purchased Mac's house. I had all four corners of that double deal!

BUYING RENTAL HOUSES

After working two jobs—Purex and real estate—I purchased a rental on Ramsey in La Mirada. It was a storybook house built by Kaufman and Broad. The second story was really a half story.

I took over an FHA loan. In those days you could take over a government loan with just a deed; the lender had no call on them. A man named Mr. Acock had purchased the four-bedroom house for his mom and dad, but the plane they were coming to California on crashed. He had the house up for sale, and I gave him $1000 or $1200 and took over his loan. That was my first rental. It cost me $13,250 and it has paid for itself many times over.

As I said earlier, our first home was on Dunrobin. Then I purchased a fixer-upper on Ringwood in Santa Fe Springs. We moved into it, and I rented out the Dunrobin house for one dollar over the payments on Ringwood—$101. We purchased this one with our own credit, an FHA mortgage with a low down payment. The rear patio had been removed to pass FHA inspection. In came a heavy rainstorm. I got up in the dark and put my foot down into an inch of water. Well, I got building permits and built a very nice new patio, and that solved that problem.

After a couple of years, we took over a loan on a house on Scribner in Whittier, moved there, and made a couple of dollars renting the Ringwood house. After a couple years in the Scribner house, we moved to Groveside Avenue, to a nice home in a nice area, and this one was already fixed up. There again I took over a low-interest VA loan and still kept my payments lower than the house I was moving out of.

By making fairly good money in my real estate sales and not raising my housing cost, I was able to invest in more rental property. In those days I subscribed to a default service, and they let me know when a foreclosure was filed. I was able to find some fairly high FHA and VA assumable loans. I had read about using other people's money and credit. Taking over these loans was a legal way to acquire wealth without using your own credit. I almost always rented the houses for enough to pay the mortgage on our family home, and I made most of the repairs myself, so I was able to keep things together. I made a few bad deals as well as some okay deals.

WORKING AT PONDOFF-SOPP REALTY

I noted that Pondoff and Sopp were the big real estate operators in Santa Fe Springs, and I decided to check them out. Nick Pondoff was the outspoken one, and Glenn the quiet one. I went to work in Glenn's office and started doing my canvassing.

Nick wanted us to get rid of a hundred cards a week or do phone work. I worked those streets over and over. The people told me lots of information about the builder, the schools, you name it. One day I was canvassing, and a lady came to the door without a stitch of clothing on. The screen was closed and I made my words short and left. I was happily married and wanted no problems.

Mario, an old insurance salesman, sat in the desk behind me, and he was a good phone man. My first six months at Pondoff-Sopp I only made $1200, but I had several in escrow and several listings. I had been planting the seeds for the harvest.

The next year we had a speaker at one of our meetings, and he asked us to write down what we wanted to make in the next year and give it to our boss. My first full year at Pondoff-Sopp, I made about $12,000. Mario made about the same.

We started attending Bethany Baptist Church. The senior pastor left and an interim came. In one sermon he challenged us to quit sitting on our wallets and give more to the Lord's work. I had been giving about ten dollars or so a week, and I doubled that. Well, at the end of the next year I made over $20,000. Not bad in the mid-60s. My last year at Pondoff-Sopp, I made more money than anyone else. Well, Mario asked what I did different— we both had the same customer base, but I made twice as much as he. All I could say was that I doubled what I gave to the Lord, and He doubled what He gave to me. I was learning that it all belongs to God.

In those days whenever the company made thirty deals, it would give a party at the Rim Ram Restaurant. Some of the sales staff got a little wild, but I kept my witness for Jesus.

Many years later, we were presenting an offer on a house. I was then on my own, and Nick came in with an offer from his client for a house we were selling. He came around the table and put his arm on my shoulder and said, "This is my boy. I taught him all he knows." We remain friends to this day. Nick was a church man, a Catholic, and he clearly loved God in his own way. Once I overheard him telling a story to a saleslady that was having a bad day. He told her that he was from Missouri, and that soon after he came to Los Angeles, he got down to his last twenty dollars. He went to church and when the offering came by, he put in a ten-dollar bill. That very evening he got in a crap game and won twenty dollars.

Sebring Construction had built about a hundred homes in Whittier, and many of them Gene Sebring had sold on land contract, with only a couple of hundred dollars down. The buyers paid Mr. Sebring directly, rather than going through a bank. They had one home which had a big water tank behind it, and they had not been able to sell the house. I wound up with the listing. I must have done a good job, as thereafter whenever one of Sebring's buyers fell far behind on his payments, Mr. Sebring—and sometimes his wife, Margie—would come out from Westwood and pick me up and we would drive by the property. If it looked bad, he would give me a quitclaim deed and ask me to see if I could get the people to sign the deed and also an agreement to give him back the property. If the property was kept up, he generally gave them a little more time. I have always been good at dealing with people and with making repairs if the people moved out. I would get the place clean and ready for the sales market. I did all that for a reduced commission, but I got his business, and later he built a few more homes in North Whittier and used my services again.

While working for Pondoff-Sopp, I started keeping an eye open for more rental property. As a result of reading Nickerson's *How I Turned $1000 into a Million in Real Estate in My Spare Time* and Napoleon Hill's *Think and Grow Rich*, I had decided to set a goal of owning fifty houses by the time I was fifty years old.

When I found a deal, I would offer it to Nick and sometimes make a deal with him for me to buy it and pay the company a reduced fee. My ninety shares of Purex were now worth enough to buy three houses. I sold a home on Buell Street to a family named Bates. They were there a couple of years when they called to ask me to buy their house because they wanted to move to Missouri. I made a deal with Nick and purchased the house, taking over their FHA loan. I rented the house out. This made House #4.

Less than a month later Jim Bates walked in the door of the office and said they were back—they never even unpacked in Missouri. He wanted me to find them a house, and he gave me some areas to look in. A day or so later I was canvassing, going door to door, and I came upon a nice home on Cedardale, which the owners wanted to sell. I told them I had a buyer, and I did—the Bates family. Well, a couple of years later, Jim Bates called and asked me to sell the Cedardale house. He said they were going to Missouri for good this time. Well, I made a deal with Nick to purchase the house and made it another rental. As far as I know, the Bates family never returned to California, but I guess they could have.

Also, while working at Pondoff-Sopp, a couple of salesmen and I purchased a house together. I later purchased their shares and rented it. That one I sold to the tenant.

I first got my salesman license, then after two years I got my broker license. Two other salesmen there wanted me to use my broker license and start a company with them. They were great men, but one of them was not a Christian, and the Bible says, "Be not unequally yoked," so I felt I had to pass on the offer. I stayed and worked for Pondoff-Sopp a few more years.

CHURCH AND OUR HOLY LAND CRUISE

During these years, we first attended Downey Baptist Church, and then when we moved to Santa Fe Springs, we moved our membership to Bethany Baptist. We were active in the young people's class, and I was often a class officer. We worked in Junior Church, where I often told the children short stories. I also worked in Royal Rangers, a young people's program. One year I was a counselor at Forest Home in their Teepee Village. We had two growing boys, Vance and Kevin. I lived with five or six boys that week. One child was from a broken home and was a wild one. One evening when we had all crawled into our sleeping bags, he called out that he had to go to the bathroom. The bathroom was down a path, so I told him to take his light. Well, in a few minutes, we heard him screaming. I ran down the hill and there he stood, shining his flashlight up into a tree, with a raccoon looking down at him. The raccoon had scared him when he ran down the trail.

In 1972 Nancy and I went on a Holy Land cruise to Israel, Syria, Greece, and Lebanon. Our pastor was our tour guide. He was part of a group led by Dr. McBurney, who was part of a school for pastors. We flew from Los Angeles, to Maine, and on to Athens, Greece. We toured the ruins of Corinth. We traveled aboard a ship, the Sunion, by night and toured by bus in the daytime, so we covered lots of places. It was a great two weeks!

One man in our group, Hal, was a cut-up. He sat behind us on the bus as we were going through Turkey. The bus stopped at a roadblock and uniformed men got on and began questioning the guides. Hal stood up and called out to them as he tapped me on the shoulder, "Here is your man. This is the one you are looking for!" This was just after the 1969 war. There were bombed-out tanks and other evidence of war all over. The soldier pulled me to the back of the bus. Nancy didn't know what to do, so she followed. The fact that I was half Syrian, with the name Nordine, caused some alarm. The tour guide finally convinced the soldier that Hal was a jokester and I was released.

We visited Jacob's Well, and it looked to me sort of like the one we used on the sharecrop farm. Somehow I dropped my green card, which was my passport entry card. If you planned to go to Syria they issued you a green card so your passport would not be stamped with entry/exit stamps from Israel, as relations between the two countries were not good. We were assigned to the King David Hotel, and someone found my green card and turned it in. God was watching over me. That was a fine hotel. It was the first time I ever saw a bidet. I was impressed and years later, when I built my home, I put one in.

I had an 8mm movie camera and took lots of footage of the trip. I later showed it at a church gathering and at the boys' school classes. You had to install the little rolls of film in the camera and remove them when they ended. Once by accident I installed a used roll and ran it through again. When I developed the film, you could see the later images as the main focus, and the earlier ones as an image in the background. It made an interesting film. Our boys stayed with their grandparents, the Fennells, while we were away. We developed several friends at Bethany Church which we still have today.

Chapter 4

The Years in My Own Business

OPENING MY OWN REAL ESTATE OFFICE

In March 1969, I rented a little building for sixty dollars a month on Whittier Boulevard in Whittier, California, and opened Nordine Realty. I had had a good four years at Pondoff-Sopp and left with their blessings. I hired a part-time secretary and had new cards and promotion material printed. The office was in the northwest part of Whittier.

At Pondoff-Sopp we used a chalkboard frame out in front to advertise a house for rent. I copied this idea and made a similar board. Whenever a person came in and asked about the house for rent, we would try to sell them a house instead. I didn't always have a house for rent, so I started putting Bible verses and godly sayings on the board—or at least on one side of the board. As the area was a little seedy, I wanted the public to know I stood with Christ. As the years went by, the "house for rent" ads were deleted and the Lord got both sides of the board.

BUILDING A BUSINESS CENTER AND OFFICE

My first little office had two rooms—one for my secretary and one for me. I did have a few salespeople who came and worked with or for me. My friend and secretary, Glenna, soon got her license and became a saleslady for my office.

I got a new secretary, Norma. She had two sons and could speak Spanish. I sold a new home to her and her husband, Marty. It was built by Sebring, and it was just a few blocks from my office. Norma was with me till I built my own business center and office on Imperial Highway in La Mirada in 1979-80. That location was not handy for her and her family, so she didn't make the move with us.

Norma asked me how I was going to pay for the new office and center. The Spirit of the Lord seemed to come to me, and I said, "Norma, ask me in two years and I will tell you how the Lord paid for the center." When it was all finished, I called Norma, took her to lunch, and told her how the Lord had supplied the money to pay for the center.

By then, the center was all done and paid for. The Lord had done it. Every time I needed to pay a subcontractor, the Lord sent a buyer for something I owned. Once it was an apartment in Long Beach. Another time it was a used motor home. It was parked in front of our house and a couple came by and asked to buy it. They had a brown paper bag full of money, and they said the Lord had directed them to it. I could hardly believe it! I rushed the cash to the bank in time to pay a bill that was due. On the last part of the project, I owed the mason $10,000 and the money was not in the bank. I knew I needed to be responsible, and I did have a line of credit, so I called my banker and asked them to put $10,000 in my account. That very afternoon, the phone rang and an agent from Caltrans (California Department of Transportation) said,

"Mr. Nordine, you know that little lot in Los Angeles that we have been haggling about?" (I had paid $525 for it.) "Yes," I said. He asked what I would take for it, and I replied, "$10,000." He said, "How about $11,450?" I knew Someone else was calling the shots! Of course I agreed.

The center is made of Mexican slump block with a red tile roof. I built a 48-foot-high western windmill on the corner and on the windmill tail, I painted "Son Light Center." A crane lifted my son Vance up in a sling, and he attached the wheel part to the mill. Vance also did the tile work in the bathrooms and entries. I paid a professional tile man to coach him.

Crown of Thorns plant like the one at my office

I designed my office after a mission church with open beams and a bay window. For my fireplace, I used a replica of the fireplace in one of the homes of Pio Pico, the last governor of California while it was still under Mexican rule.

We visited the Crystal Cathedral about that time and noted a lovely flowering cactus. The guide told us it was a Crown of Thorns, which is believed to be the plant used to make the crown of thorns the soldiers put on Christ Jesus when they crucified him. I planted one near the chalkboard and my door. It has been beautiful for thirty years now.

I prayed for a certain mix of tenants for the center, and the Lord gave me the mix almost to a tee.

MY CHALKBOARD MINISTRY

When I finished the center, I put up my two 3' x 7' chalkboards and wrote on them, "THANKS LORD AND CUSTOMERS FOR MY NEW CENTER." An elderly Jewish man had often come by the building project to chat with me. After I put up my boards, my friend told me that it was not good to mix religion and business. But I was able to tell him how the Lord had supplied.

Over the years, I have published on the chalkboards Scripture verses, godly sayings, and messages that I felt God had given me. I have had people express their appreciation for the words they read on the boards.

One such person occasionally came into the office when I was not there and left little gifts for me and my family, many with Scripture verses on them. However, I never had the opportunity to meet him. This continued on and off for a number of years, and finally he left a gift with a note and his name. Sometime later I was in the office when he came in. Somehow I just knew he was my elusive friend. We had a special visit and prayer together. He told me that he had done phone work across the street some years before and the message on the board had spoken to his heart.

Another person, a lady, came into the office and told my secretary how reading the board had caused her to give up drug use and turn her life around.

For pictures of the chalkboard messages, please see the photo section at the end of the book.

FAMILY AND CHURCH

In the first few years of our young boys' lives, we moved several times, but about the time our younger son, Kevin, started to school, we purchased our home on Groveside Avenue in Whittier.

We stayed there for sixteen years while Vance and Kevin went to school. They helped me by passing out flyers and cards for my real estate business. I paid them, and they paid half of their fees to attend church school. We were active in church, and that was a good part of our social lives. I was never a big sports person, but I did attend some of our sons' little league games. Vance, our oldest, did cross country in high school. He attended Biola University. He is like me, a natural mechanic, but also good at art and his major was art. He met his wife, Gloria, there, and they have given me three wonderful grandchildren—Mary, Rose, and Wesley. Our son Kevin attended California State University at Fullerton and Bob Jones University. He now has a very successful career in the mortgage industry.

We attended Whittier Hills Baptist Church for about seventeen years while our children were growing up. For the last ten years or so, we have split our church-going between several fine churches. We now have a second home at Silver Lakes in Helendale, California, on the lake, and we have attended a couple of fine churches when we are there, which is quite often.

MOVING AND REBUILDING HOUSES

I have been building and fixing things most all my life, especially since I started in the real estate business. I have moved twelve houses from one location to another and prepared them to sell or rent. When the path was being cleared to build the 105 freeway, I purchased thirteen houses in one day and moved eleven of them.

One of them didn't pencil out; in other words, I decided it wouldn't be profitable to move. So I hired a couple of men and got a big roll-off bin. We tore the house down with picks and hammers and loaded it in the bin. I had to post a $5000 bond to have the house off the lot by a certain date. As we were working, a policeman came by and saw us and ordered us to stop and sit down. I showed him the paperwork, and he finally said, "Okay, go back to work."

I am sure we looked pretty dumb buying a house and then tearing it down and putting it in a dumpster. I won some and lost some, but I did okay overall on those move-ons. I still own four homes I moved in the 70s, and they have been good income rentals. I took ten-year loans on some of them and thirty-year loans on some. We now have them all paid off.

Once in a house-moving project, I was going to streamline the project. I got a backhoe man to dig the foundation. We poured the lower part of the foundation and planned to form the top when the house was moved over the lower part. Well, the Lord sent some very heavy rain, and red clay mud covered the lower part. We had a big clean-up job to do! The house was a big one and we had to cut it in two to move it, but it turned out fine and we sold it.

I had a contractor named Harry doing my north area move-ons. He would move his house trailer onto the job lot, hook up to my electricity and water, and do the work for me. One house I did in Altadena was a turnkey, meaning it was ready to sell when we finished it. Harry did the complete job for a fixed price. I did some of the houses in the southern area, and when I ran behind, I called Harry and he would come and help me.

Once when Harry was sitting in my little office on the boulevard, he said to me, "I like to do a pretty job as cheap as I can." Well, a house in Altadena sure brought back those words. A year or so after I listed it and another broker sold it, I got a call from the selling agent. Her clients had called her because the living room ceiling fell down. Those words of Harry rang in my ears. I asked if they wanted their money back or the ceiling redone, and they wanted it repaired; they liked their home. My son Vance took a crew up and redid the ceilings. The house was an older one, with lath and plaster walls, and moving it for twenty-five miles must have broken the plaster loose from the wood laths.

When I did that move-on project, the market was in a low curve. I sold the little house for $49,000 and the sale fell apart. The people rented it for one year and moved out. Then I listed it for $59,000, and it sold quickly—the market was on an upswing. I have found that in the down markets, it's wise to do building projects, and in the up markets, it's best to sell or rent. I have been more of a "buy and keep," but I sold about half of the move-ons within a couple of years.

BUILDING INTO LIVES

I purchased a rental in La Habra and rented it to a carpenter, Tony, and his wife. Since I did a good deal of building, Tony and I became friends and he gave me good carpenter advice. For instance, once I was holding an open house for sale and Tony came by. The house had been built by an architect. It had eight-foot, two-inch doors that all dragged when opening and closing. Tony showed me a trick of the trade, how to make a simple adjustment and correct the problem.

One evening about eight or nine, the phone rang; this was when we had only landlines. It was Tony's wife. She was upset and proceeded to tell me that Tony was drunk and had passed out, and that she was afraid of him. I said, "If he has passed out, he certainly will not hurt you. I will come over in the morning."

The next day when I went over, Tony was up. I sat down on the couch and told Tony he needed help. I asked if he would like to ask Jesus to forgive his sins and come into his life. He said yes, he would. He prayed, and I asked his wife if she would like to ask Jesus into her life, too. She declined.

About this time Tony was out of work and got behind on his rent. I had led him to the Lord and I wanted to help him, so I let the rent slide for some time. But I finally felt I needed to make a decision. I had a second trust deed on the house and it was coming due. I recall thinking, "I will call the holder of the second, and if he will extend the loan for a year or two, I will let Tony slide."

I called the holder, and as I started to ask about the extension, he broke in and said he had been thinking about calling me and asking if I needed an extension! So I gave Tony more time and more time, and one day he came in and paid it all up. He said he got a big check from the carpenters union.

Sometime later Tony asked my advice. His wife was sick and in a convalescent hospital, and he had a lady friend that he liked very much. Should he divorce his sick wife and marry this lady? I gave him some words from the Bible and he waited. In a year or so his wife passed and he then married his new friend. He came in and thanked me for guiding him in the right direction.

THE HOLDUP

I hired a Christian contractor to do the south move-on houses. They were young men with a license, but their work lacked quality, and I finally had to let them go and finish the job myself. I never questioned their faith, but their work as contractors was not up to my expectations.

One of the houses I took over to finish on 99th in Los Angeles was in a poor area. The elderly couple next door were good Christian folks and even brought me lunch. But once when I was at the property, another couple came and wanted to see the house. It was boarded up as it was not finished, but I took them in.

The house where I was held up

When I entered the back part, the man stepped behind me and, in a wink, put a police nelson on me, wrapping his arm around my neck and holding a knife to my throat. They went through my pockets and took my thirty dollars. Then the man pulled my glasses off. I told him I needed them to drive. I guess I was being optimistic for a man with a knife at his throat, but he replied, "I will leave them on your car. Just stay back here for ten minutes and you won't get hurt." I took his advice and when I went out, the glasses were on my car.

I was a bit shaken up, but a few days later I went to the police station to make a report and look at the mug books. To my surprise, the duty officer behind the desk looked like the holdup man! I didn't know what to make of that. I looked at the mug shots, found one that looked like him, and left. Maybe three days later I got a call. The caller said he was from the Los Angeles Police Department. He said the suspected robber had been shot and killed in another holdup, so I should feel at ease. Well, I wasn't too sure about that!

FINANCING AND BANKING

Several times over the years I have sold homes and carried a mortgage, sometimes a second trust deed and note. The Lord has given me wisdom in that area, I guess, as I have never lost a lot of money doing that.

I know the housing mess the real estate industry got into in 2005-2012 could have been avoided if people had studied the real estate curve over the years. For example, I sold a home and carried a second trust deed on it. The interest was 10 percent. I told the buyer that if they ran into financial problems to keep up with their payments to the bank on their first mortgage and let me slide on the second (in other words, not to pay me until they were able).

There was a housing recession and the man called me. I confirmed that I would wait on payment and waive the first five years' interest on the second trust deed. I told him to keep up the payments to the bank on the first mortgage. Well, he did, and in five more years real estate values had swung up. He was able to sell at a profit and pay me off. I didn't make the 10 percent on the first five years, but I did on the last five. The buyer didn't lose their home and I made a profit also.

When all parties work together, you can generally work out a fair solution to a financial problem. So many problems are caused by selfishness and greed on the part of all parties.

I mentioned earlier that I had a line of credit at the bank. I used it for my guaranteed sales and equity purchases. My contractor had made enough to buy himself some lots in Pomona, but not enough to build houses on them, so he talked me into going to my bank and trying to help him get some financing. I recall my banker telling me that he was sorry, but he had to say no to my friend. He said the contractor pretty much worked alone, and what if he broke his leg? How would he make his loan payments?

Well I borrowed $30,000 and lent it to my friend. I had long since finished my move-on project and was busy selling houses. My friend's loan came due. (Normally I only borrowed funds for ninety days, or sometimes up to six months.) I went out to Pomona looking for the contractor. His houses were not finished, and I found him at the VA hospital. His diabetes had gotten out of control and he had lost the use of his arms. Once again words of wisdom rang in my ears: "What if he breaks his leg and can't pay?"

In time he recovered. He finished and sold his houses and paid me back, but I had to dig into my personal money to carry him for some time. I normally took trust deeds on any money I loaned to customers, so in due time I was paid back, but sometimes it took a while. I have been a risk taker most of my life, but I try to measure the risk and keep a sure footing and lean on Jesus. My wife says sometimes I keep Him busy.

FORECLOSURE GONE BAD—SLA LOCKOUT

One of those bad deals was a trust deed sale I went to at the courthouse in Norwalk. I had gotten information about a house in Rowland Heights. The price was $50,000, which was a good deal; the property was worth $80,000 to $90,000. I showed up and bid $50,000. A young lady came up to me and told me not to bid. She pulled out a gold coin and bid something, but the auctioneer paid no attention to her.

I was the high bidder, and when I went to see the property, guess who was living there. The young lady! I did some investigating and discovered that the property had gone to a prior sale and she had made the same bid. She had then gone to the house and told the owners she had purchased the house. She gave the owners some cash and helped them move nearby. She and her dad moved in, even though it wasn't their house.

In a couple of days I got a call at the office. The lady on the phone asked if I was the new owner. I said, "Yes," and she said, "Are you sitting down?"

I sat down, and she explained there was a $40,000 additional loan on the house. Well, it turned out to cost me $90,000—top dollar. Plus I had to evict the young woman and her dad. The woman drove a Jeep Renegade and lived the part. They dodged the process server, whom I knew.

In my after-the-fact investigation, I met the former owners and heard their story. I had an extra copy of the eviction papers in my case when I went out to check on the property. The former owner, whom the young woman had made friends with, came by on a bicycle. She was chatting with me when the young woman came wheeling in and jumped out of the jeep. She came over and said, "What's up, guys?"

We made light talk for a few minutes and she excused herself.

I turned and said to the older woman, "Would you like to make twenty dollars?" I handed her the papers and she called out to the younger woman and handed her the papers. She had just been outdone! She had been served.

It turned out that she and her dad were in a movement like the SLA (Symbionese Liberation Army). They considered themselves freedom fighters and were trying to get attention in the courts and the press. The woman wrote a long answer to the complaint, saying that she had rejected her citizenship. The court rejected their answer, and we got a judgment for possession. They were both gone when the marshal came, cut the locks, and walked through the house. He told me to change the locks.

I got a couple of men to help me move all the people's stuff into the attached garage. We found several boxes of ammunition and several guns, one being a rifle on a tripod in a case, a nearly new weapon. We put all the guns and ammunition in Nancy's car trunk. She was a bit wary that she would get stopped with all those weapons. I posted a note for the evicted people telling them that they could come get their belongings. They came and picked up their things, with the exception of the weapons.

I took the weapons to the sheriff's station, but they would not take them. They checked their records and said the weapons had not been reported stolen. When I set the tripod AR-15 on the counter, the sheriff put his hand on his pistol and told me to put the weapon away.

The evicted tenant, the father, came over to my office and picked up the weapons. He told me they were in a movement to save America from the corrupt government. The people in their movement felt the government was taking the wrong path and they wanted to get publicity to save the country. I tried to tell them about Jesus, but he said they were religious. I never got a conversion for Jesus, but I got the property.

This was a difficult purchase, but I win some and lose some. This one made memories. When I see a Jeep Renegade, I still think of that young woman.

ANOTHER TOUGH ONE

Last year about June, rent from one of my homes in Joshua Tree failed to arrive on time. I had rented the home to two elderly men. One was a diabetic and had lost his legs. The other had a knitting business. I am not sure who did the knitting. They had three or four dogs and cats—too many. They had been pretty good payers, but the one with the knitting business had been in and out of the hospital with a heart condition.

When the rent didn't come in, I took a drive out and found a big pile of debris in the driveway and a bigger one in the garage. The door was open so I went in. The furniture was still there, but the place looked ransacked. I set out to find what had happened to them.

After much investigation, I finally called the coroner's office. Yes, I was told, they came out and picked up one of them on June 15th. I finally heard from the other man's daughter-in-law. He had died two weeks earlier. They had taken what they wanted and had no intention of coming back to clean up or dispose of the junk. The animals were all gone, but the stink was terrible.

The two men had a library with all sorts of books. One of my other tenants who lives nearby helps out at the library, and he suggested I donate the books to Joshua Tree Library, which I did. I was impressed by the books on the nightstand. I saw *90 minutes in Heaven* by Don Piper, *Glimpses of Heaven* by Trudy Harris, *A Closer Walk with Jesus, Guideposts, Crossing the Threshold of Eternity* by Robert Wise, and *The Day I Died* by Steve Sjogren.

While I was there, the house phone rang. I answered it and the caller asked for Ben, saying she was his friend. I told her the story as best I knew, and she asked what had happened to the twelve cats. (Twelve! I had no idea there were that many.) I replied that there were no animals there when we came.

We hauled many loads to thrift shops, a church store and the dump. We took the artificial legs to a place the county hospital directed us to. That was a job I will never forget.

It was a big job putting that house back in shape, but we finally did and rented it again.

Chapter 5

Recent Years

MEETING A PRESIDENT

In January of 2006 Nancy and I received an invitation to go to a Carter Center event at the UCLA Cove. We had given a donation to the Carter Center, and that is most likely why we were given an invitation to meet with the former President, Jimmy Carter.

I have read many of President Carter's books and have been greatly impressed with his Christian testimony. I took a copy of one of his books with me to ask him to sign it.

I guess we were a bit excited as we got our dates mixed up and went a day early, so we had to go back again on the right day.

Well, on that special day, there were briefings of the Carter Center work, a luncheon, and a time to visit and have our pictures taken with the former President. We went to the briefings and learned how the Center helps in third world countries, in health, elections, and home building.

My favorite memories of the day include lunch in the Cove at the same table as the couple who sponsored the dinner and a chance meeting in the hall with Mr. Carter, who greeted me graciously. I also enjoyed the opportunity to have our picture taken with Mr. Carter.

We went out on the balcony to greet the President, and as we waited in line I noted all the secret service men with their shiny black shoes. When it was our turn to speak to the President, I asked if he would sign his book for me. He said, "I don't have a pen."

I handed him a company pen and he signed my book; of course I gave him the pen!

He asked what I liked about the book.

I said, "The part where you and Evangelist Cruz went door to door telling people about Jesus and you asked Cruz how it was that when he talked to the people they seemed to respond better than when you spoke to them. And Cruz said, 'First you love God and second you love that person in front of you.'"

Jimmy thanked me. The crowd heard the two secrets of Christian love. It was great to meet a leader who loves Jesus.

**Nancy and me with former President Jimmy
Carter at the Carter Event UCLA**

AND HERE I AM TODAY (December 2013)

Since I gave my son Vance my client list a few years ago, I have kept pretty busy with my property management. Bea was my assistant for over twenty-five years. She has since retired and I have hired another secretary to take her place. God has been good to me and I am grateful. At seventy-six, I am slowing down some.

Nancy, my wife of fifty-four years, has been at my side to assist me in my projects for fun and work. Her family became my family. We lost her dad, Howard, last year. Her mother, Stella, is doing well at a retirement center. We go down to visit and dine with her often. She is a great lady at ninety-four and counting.

I have supported fifteen to twenty missionaries or mission works for most of my adult life. When we built our home on Avocado Crest Road in La Habra Heights, we included a room where we could invite missionaries to stay. God doesn't have a short arm.

One joy I have had is leading people through the plan of salvation to Jesus. Some things are too good not to share! I have been outspoken and that includes sharing my love of God. I have led people all around me to Jesus, plus using two 3' x 7' chalkboards for forty years to give out His Word.

Not long ago I visited a home we own in Pico Rivera. The neighbor came out to tell me her dad had passed away. It was a sad-happy day. I had led him through the plan of salvation several years back. I was sad to know he was gone, but happy I had presented the way to Jesus and he had accepted Him. Those are my joy times, serving my Lord Jesus.

FORTY YEARS OF CHALKBOARD MESSAGES

As I said earlier, I began giving out the Gospel through messages on a chalkboard shortly after I opened my first real estate office on

Whittier Boulevard in Whittier. From 1970 to 1979 the messages pointed the way to God from there. Then I moved the office, and since then, the messages have been displayed on Imperial Highway in La Mirada. I am still posting them there, and I have begun to post them on FaceBook as well.

About 30,000 vehicles go by my office each day, so I pray a few will see my signs and the signs will point them to Jesus. Some people do object to my witness sign. They have poured paint on it, pulled it down, and thrown eggs on it, but I just clean it up and keep on giving out the Word.

Once, someone threw red paint all over it. Well, I just left it there for a while and I wrote on it, "Christ's blood paid for your sins and my sins." I felt they would want to show their buddies. I do get some positive feedback and just hope I meet a few folks in glory who are there because the sign pointed the way.

Below is a story about my chalkboard ministry that my friend Dr. Don Watson included in his publication *"And You Visited Me."* Following that I have included photos of many of the messages that appeared on my chalkboard over the years. As you read them over, I pray they will encourage your heart and inspire you to share them with others. To God be the glory.

"And You Visited Me"

Diversified Christian Ministries, Inc

Dr. Don E. Watson, President

P.O. Box 1370   Carlsbad, CA 92018-1370

A Roadside Witness For Christ!

Donald Nordine of La Habra Heights, California, has been a faithful friend of DCM and a member of our "DCM Support Team" for the entire 28 years of our existence! He has a real estate office located on Imperial Hiway where 30,000 vehicles pass by each Day!

So, for the past 40 years Don has used the chalk board in front of his office to share a message of hope and salvation in the Lord Jesus Christ. 40 years!! Can you imagine the positive Christian and Biblical influence upon the thousands upon thousands of occupants of the cars, taxis and busses that pass by on Imperial Hiway <u>every day</u>! Don, I'm proud of you! Keep up the good witness!

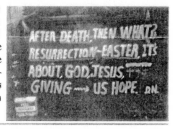

From *"And You Visited Me,"* a publication of Dr. Don E. Watson, president of Diversified Christian Ministries, Inc.

Chalkboard Photo Section

REJOICE MOMS, GOD GAVE U AN IMPORTANT JOB, TO GUIDE THE CHILDREN TO JESUS. D.N.

SPECIALS

WHEN, YOU SEEK GOD, WITH ALL YOUR HEART, JESUS FINDS U, & HIS LOVE WILL NEVER LET U GO. D.N.

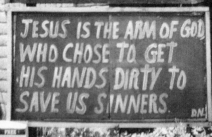

JESUS IS THE ARM OF GOD, WHO CHOSE TO GET HIS HANDS DIRTY TO SAVE US SINNERS. D.N.

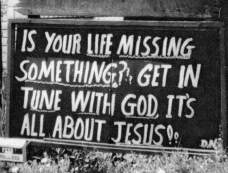

INTEGRITY,→LIVING BY JESUS' RULES (BEYOND THE CROWD) EVEN WHEN IT IS DIFFICULT. TE-DN

REAL ESTATE

WHEN, GOD'S LOVE IN US, IS OVERFLOWING, WE HAVE NO ROOM 4 HATE, KILLING & WAR

JESUS (GOD) CAME TO GIVE US A NEW WAY, LOVE, GOD & YOUR NEIGHBOR.

PALMS SUNDAY!!! HOORAY.
GOOD FRIDAY?!: TROUBLE!
DON'T ABANDON JESUS,
HE IS LORD.
D.N.

SPECIALS

"FOCUS ON GOD's LOVE."
LORD,! OPEN THE EYES
OF OUR HEARTS + LET
US SEE JESUS."
D.N.

HAS SIN___,___GOT A GRIP
ON YOU?; REPENT + ASK
JESUS (GOD) TO FREE U.
D.N.

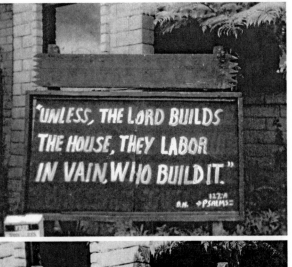

"UNLESS, THE LORD BUILDS THE HOUSE, THEY LABOR IN VAIN, WHO BUILD IT."
D.N. PSALMS 127:1

WE ALL FAIL, + NEED A SAVIOR, JESUS SAYS, "COME UNTO ME."
D.N.

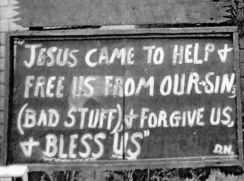

"JESUS CAME TO HELP + FREE US FROM OUR SIN, (BAD STUFF) + FORGIVE US, + BLESS US"
D.N.

SPECIALS
O' LORD, BE OUR VISION,
DEEP DOWN IN OUR
SOUL, LET US SEEK THEE,
AS OUR GUIDE.
D.N.

REAL ESTATE
TRY GOING (GOD's) JESUS'
WAY. LIFE'S ROAD IS TOO
ROUGH TO GO IT ALONE.
WRAP YOURSELF IN GOD.
D.N.

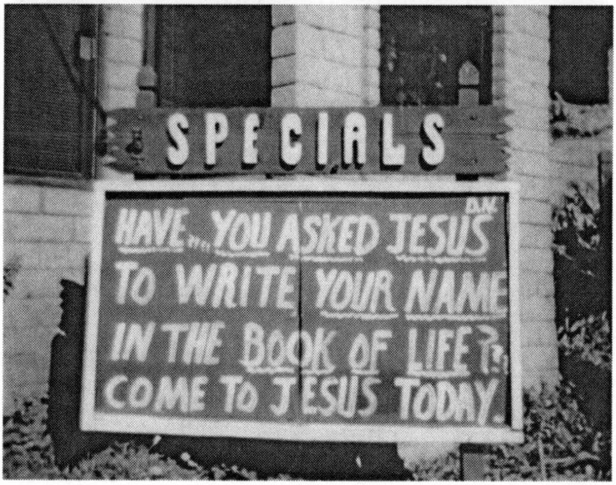
SPECIALS
D.N.
HAVE... YOU ASKED JESUS
TO WRITE YOUR NAME
IN THE BOOK OF LIFE?
COME TO JESUS TODAY.

REAL ESTATE

"TELL THE DEVIL TO GET LOST." "ASK JESUS TO RUN YOUR LIFE, & BECOME A CHILD OF GOD."

REAL ESTATE

"LET ALL THINGS BE DONE IN (LOVE) CHARITY"

S.PAUL I: CORINTHIANS 16:4 d1.

REAL ESTATE

LOVE & SERVICE 4 GOD & OTHERS. "LET THIS MIND BE N U, WHICH WAS IN CHRIST JESUS." PHIL 2:5

SPECIALS

CHRISTMAS, GOD, SENDING
A SAVIOR TO GUIDE HIS
LOST CHILDREN HOME.
RECEIVE CHRIST AS SAVIOR & GUIDE

REAL ESTATE

THE GIFT OF LOVE, IS
THE GREATEST GIFT,
GIVE IT GENEROUSLY,
LOVE GOD & OTHERS

SPECIALS

THANKS LORD 4 GIVING
US JESUS, TO LOVE &
TO BRING US INTO YOUR
FAMILY TREE. †

REAL ESTATE

LIFE IS SO UNCERTAIN!
LIVE FOR JESUS TODAY.

"FAIRWELL-GOOD-BY- DAN HOVIS."
D.N.

"COMMIT THY WAY(LIFE)UNTO
THE LORD(JESUS): TRUST ALSO
IN HIM; & HE SHALL
BRING IT TO PASS."
PS:37:5

FREE
BROCHURES

"LIFE IS ABOUT CHOICES,
CHOOSE TO FOLLOW
JESUS, ALWAYS, WHAT
WOULD JESUS DO?"
D.N.

FREE
BROCHURES

HOLD THE DOOR OPEN
4 JESUS, (GOD) & DON'T
LET THE WORLD BLOW
IT SHUT.
MAKE JESUS *1. D.N.

GOD's LOVE IN US,
CAUSES ACTION, IT'S
TOO GOOD NOT TO SHARE
TAKE ACTION, LIVE 4 JESUS.
D.N.

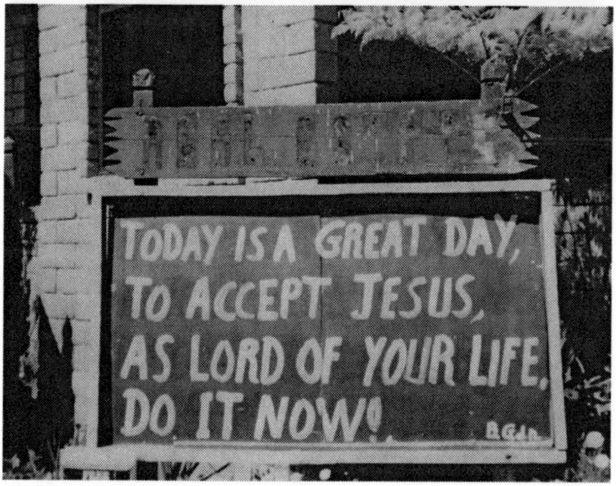
TODAY IS A GREAT DAY,
TO ACCEPT JESUS,
AS LORD OF YOUR LIFE.
DO IT NOW!
B.G.D.

REAL ANSWERS

JESUS' LIFE & DEATH, SAYS, "I AM THE ONE, WHO LOVES YOU."

BE TAGMANN

REAL ANSWERS

LIVE ON THE EDGE FOR JESUS, EVEN WHEN U DON'T KNOW THE OUT-COME?, GOD WILL B WITH U

REAL ANSWERS

BELIEVING & FOLLOWING JESUS GIVES PURPOSE TO OUR LIVES.

DN

PROVERBS FROM THE BIBLE

THE FEAR OF THE LORD IS THE BEGINNING OF KNOWLEDGE, BUT FOOLS DESPISE WISDOM & DISCIPLINE.

SPECIALS

THE 4TH CELEBRATION IS OVER, MAKE JESUS LORD & CELEBRATE YOU, VICTORY IN JESUS. D.N.

MAY THIS ROAD SIGN POINT YOU TO JESUS. GIVE JESUS A RIDE. D.N.

SPECIALS

RENEW YOUR MIND,
FILL IT WITH (GOD).
CHRIST'S TEACHINGS.
MEMORIZE HIS WORD

SPECIALS

FAITH. KNOWING,
GOD'S HAND.
WILL NOT EVER,
LET YOU GO. D.N.

REAL ESTATE

BECAUSE CHRIST AROSE,
WE HAVE...
FORGIVENESS
FOR YESTERDAY,
STRENGTH FOR TODAY,
HOPE FOR TOMORROW

BLESS THE LORD, O MY SOUL! + ALL THAT IS WITH IN ME, BLESS HIS HOLY NAME. PSMS:103:1

HANG OUT WITH JESUS, THE COMPANY U KEEP, WILL INFECT YOU. DN

MOTHERS, TEACH YOUR CHILDREN TO "LOVE GOD + THEIR FELLOWMAN." NN.SE.Jn.

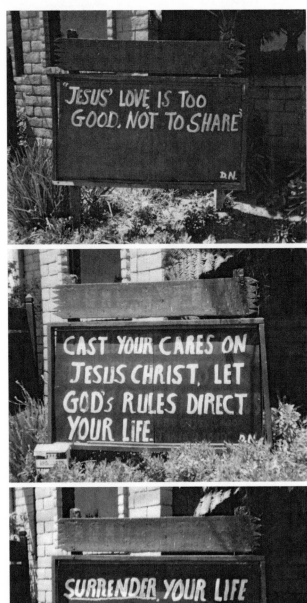

SPECIALS

GOD ALLOWS RAIN +
PAIN, BOTH CAN BE
USEFULL FOR GROWTH.
D.N.

REAL ESTATE

MAKE THE COMMIT→
MENT, MAKE CHRIST
LORD OF YOUR LIFE.
D.N.

REAL ESTATE

TRUST CHRIST
+ GOD WILL HELP
YOU PEDDLE UP
LIFE'S MOUNTAINS. *D.N.*

THEY LABOR IN VAIN,
WHO BUILD., UNLESS THE
LORD GUARDS THE CITY.

SPECIALS

CHRIST OFFERS FOR-
GIVENESS TO THOSE
THAT REPENT + FOLLOW
HIM. (LIVE GOD's WAY)

"JESUS LOVES ME (U), THIS
I KNOW, BECAUSE THE
BIBLE TELLS ME SO."

OLD Hym. N.N. dn.

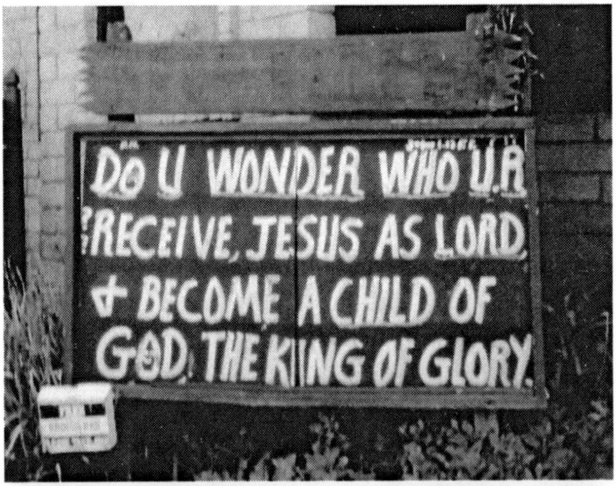
D.N.
DO U WONDER WHO U.R
RECEIVE, JESUS AS LORD,
+ BECOME A CHILD OF
GOD, THE KING OF GLORY.

SPECIALS
D.N.
THE RACE OF LIFE, IS
NOT ALWAYS WON BY
SPEED, BUT, TAKING A
TIME, 4 GOD, + LOVING JESUS.

PRAY 4 JAPAN
GIVE$ TO HELP JAPAN.
IN JESUS's NAME
D.N.

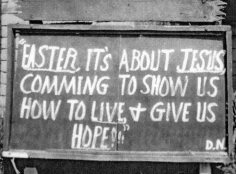

REAL ESTATE

"TELL THE DEVIL TO GET LOST." "ASK JESUS TO RUN YOUR LIFE, & BECOME A CHILD OF GOD." D.N.

SPECIALS

"PUT ON JESUS LIKE AN OVERCOAT, & LET HIS WORDS COVER YOU FROM HEAD TO TOE." D.N.

"EASTER, IT'S ABOUT JESUS COMMING TO SHOW US HOW TO LIVE, & GIVE US HOPE!!" D.N.

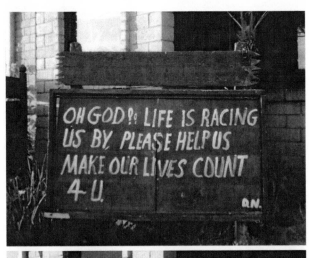

OH GOD?! LIFE IS RACING US BY, PLEASE HELP US MAKE OUR LIVES COUNT 4 U.

D.N.

ON FЬ

IS JESUS CALLING?!, COME WALK THE LINE 4 ME?!!!!, + DON'T LOOK BACK. "I'LL WALK THE LINE 4 JESUS."

D.N.

ON FЬ

GOD GIVES US LIFE 2 MAKE A DIFFERENCE, USE IT 4 JESUS (GOD) OR THE DEVIL WILL ROB U OF IT"

D.N.

SPECIALS

OUR FATHER, IN HEAVEN—
—FORGIVE US "R SINS, AS
WE FORGIVE, THOSE
THAT HAVE WRONGED US"

ON FЬ

R LIVES R LIKE A PUZZLE,
WE PUT N THE PIECES,
WHEN IT IS FINISHED,
WILL, IT GLORIFY, GOD?!

ON FЬ

IF U ENJOY LIFES PERKS?
TELL GOD, THANKS, PRAISE
IF U APPRECIATE, SOMEONE,
ACT ON IT. TELL EM. D.N.

REAL ESTATE

THE GIFT OF LOVE, IS
THE GREATEST GIFT,
GIVE IT GENEROUSLY,
LOVE GOD & OTHERS.   D.N.

SPECIALS

O' LORD, BE OUR VISION,
DEEP DOWN IN OUR
SOUL, LET US SEEK THEE,
AS OUR GUIDE.   D.N.

"LET JESUS DIRECT
YOUR LIFE. GOD KNOWS
BEST."   D.N.

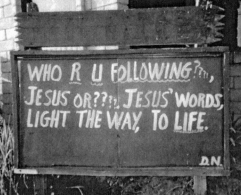

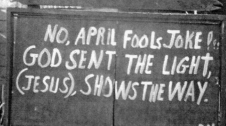

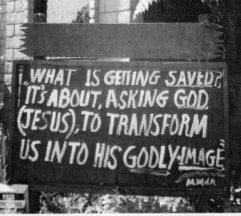

"WHAT IS GETTING SAVED? IT'S ABOUT, ASKING GOD (JESUS), TO TRANSFORM US INTO HIS GODLY-IMAGE"
M.Wdn

SPECIALS

CHRISTMAS: GOD, SENDING A SAVIOR TO GUIDE HIS LOST CHILDREN HOME. RECEIVE CHRIST AS SAVIOR+GUIDE
D.N.

"LORD HELP US, LIVE, SO R LIVES R A DISCIPLINED LOVE OFFERING, 2 U."
D.N.

SPECIALS

CHOICES?!, U CHOOSE?!?, FOLLOW CHRIST'S WAY, → (LOVE GOD & OTHERS) OR → FOLLOW THE WORLD'S WAY

D.N.

WHEN U SERVE GOD, YOU'RE A TREASURE 2 GOD & ALL GOD'S FAMILY.

D.N.

(SINNER TO SAINT)
JESUS, THE TRANSFORMER, SAYS, "FOLLOW ME, TO THE ETERNAL TREASURE OF LIFE, NOW, & HERE AFTER."

Romans 3:23-24
"…for all have sinned and fall short of the glory of God, and all are justified freely by his grace through the redemption that came by Christ Jesus."

John 3:16
"For God so loved the world that he gave his one and only Son, that whoever believes in him shall not perish but have eternal life."

Romans 10:9-10
"If you declare with your mouth, 'Jesus is Lord,' and believe in your heart that God raised him from the dead, you will be saved. For it is with your heart that you believe and are justified, and it is with your mouth that you profess your faith and are saved."

CPSIA information can be obtained at www.ICGtesting.com
Printed in the USA
BVOW07s1825280914

368555BV00001B/2/P